ROMANESQUE SCULPTURE
OF THE PILGRIMAGE ROADS

ROMANESQUE SCULPTURE
OF THE PILGRIMAGE ROADS

BY

A. KINGSLEY PORTER

IN TEN VOLUMES

VOLUME VII
ILLUSTRATIONS
WESTERN FRANCE

REPRINTED BY
HACKER ART BOOKS
NEW YORK
1969

FIRST PUBLISHED
1 9 2 3

Library of Congress Catalog Card Number 67-4262

Printed in the United States of America

ILLUSTRATIONS

(896–1138)

WESTERN FRANCE

896. AZAY-LE-RIDEAU, (Indre-et-Loire). Reliefs in western façade. Christ and twelve Apostles. L. W. P. phot.

897. CHINON, (Indre-et-Loire), St.-Mesme. Relief in ancient façade. The Crucifixion. L. W. P. phot. from a cast.

898. AIRVAULT, (Deux-Sèvres). Spandrel of nave arcade. F. M. S. phot.

899. AIRVAULT, (Deux-Sèvres). Spandrel of nave arcade. B. A. phot.

900. AIRVAULT, (Deux-Sèvres). Clerestory wall and vaulting capital. Feast at Emmaus; two Saints. F. M. S. phot.

901. AIRVAULT, (Deux-Sèvres). Capital of nave. Temptation; Adam and Eve reproved. F. M. S. phot.

902. AIRVAULT, (Deux-Sèvres). Capital of nave. F. M. S. phot.

903. AIRVAULT, (Deux-Sèvres). Tomb of the abbot Pierre de Saine-Fontaine, † 1110. L. W. P. phot.

904. CHAUVIGNY, (Vienne), St.-Pierre. Capital of ambulatory. Babylon; the Shepherds. Stoedtner phot.

905. CHAUVIGNY, (Vienne), St.-Pierre. Capital of ambulatory. Adoration of the Magi. Signed by Joffre. A. K. P. phot.

906. SAINTES, (Charente-Inférieure), Musée Archéologique. Capital. Three Apostles, St. Luke. A. K. P. phot.

907. POITIERS, (Vienne), Ste.-Radegonde. Relief now in vestibule. Christ. L. W. P. phot.

908. POITIERS, (Vienne), Ste.-Radegonde. Relief now in vestibule. Ste.-Radegonde. L. W. P. phot.

909. POITIERS, (Vienne), Ste.-Radegonde. Capital of ambulatory. Daniel and Habakkuk. F. M. S. phot.

910. POITIERS, (Vienne), Ste.-Radegonde. Capital of ambulatory. God, Adam and Eve. F. M. S. phot.

911. POITIERS, (Vienne), Ste.-Radegonde. Capital of ambulatory. F. M. S. phot.

912. POITIERS, (Vienne), St.-Hilaire. Relief in transept gable. F. M. S. phot. from cast.

913. POITIERS, (Vienne), St.-Hilaire. Capital now in Musée des Antiquaires de l'Ouest. F. M. S. phot.

914. POITIERS, (Vienne), St.-Hilaire. Relief in transept gable. F. M. S. phot. from cast.

915. POITIERS, (Vienne), St.-Hilaire. Capital. Death of St. Hilaire. F. M. S. phot. from cast.

916. La Lande de Fronzac, (Gironde). Southern portal. The apocalyptic Vision. L. W. P. phot.

917. La Lande de Fronzac, (Gironde). Tympanum of southern portal. The apocalyptic Vision. L. W. P. phot.

918. Saintes, (Charente-Inférieure), St.-Eutrope. Capital of nave. Psychostasy. B.-A. phot.

919. St.-Symphorien, (Charente-Inférieure). Western façade, portal. L. W. P. phot.

920. Bordeaux, (Gironde), Ste.-Croix. Western portal, voussure. Angels, Elders. L. W. P. phot.

921. Bordeaux, (Gironde), Ste.-Croix. Western façade, southern lunette. Five Representations of the Vice of Luxury. L. W. P. phot.

922. Angers, (Maine-et-Loire), Eglise du Ronceray. Capital in Musée Archéologique. Entry into Jerusalem. L. W. P. phot

923. Fontevrault, (Maine-et-Loire), Abbaye. Capital. *Majestas Domini;* the Assumption. B.-A. phot.

924. Parthenay-le-Vieux, (Deux-Sèvres). Western façade, northern lunette. Constantine. L. W. P. phot.

925. Parthenay-le-Vieux, (Deux-Sèvres). Western façade, southern lunette. Samson. L. W. P. phot.

926. Castelvieil, (Gironde). Southern portal, detail of voussures. L. W. P. phot.

927. Castelvieil, (Gironde). Southern portal, detail of voussures. Psychomachia. L. W. P. phot.

928. Castelvieil, (Gironde). Southern portal, detail. L. W. P. phot.

929. Angoulême, (Charente), Cathédrale. Western façade, central portion, upper zone. *Majestas Domini*, Angels, Saints. L. W. P. phot.

930. Angoulême, (Charente), Cathédrale. Western façade, central portion, fifth zone. St. Mark, St. Luke, Saints, Angels. L. W. P. phot.

931. Angoulême, (Charente), Cathédrale. Western façade, southern half, fourth and fifth zones. Prophets, Apostles, Vices (?). B.-A. phot

932. Angoulême, (Charente), Cathédrale. Western façade, northern half, fourth and fifth zones. Prophets, Vices (?), an Apostle, St. Peter. B.-A. phot.

933. Angoulême, (Charente), Cathédrale. Western façade, northern side, fourth zone. St. Peter, an Apostle. Stoedtner phot.

934. Angoulême, (Charente), Cathédrale. Western façade, northern portion, third zone. Three Apostles. L. W. P. phot.

935. Angoulême, (Charente), Cathédrale. Western façade, southern side, third zone. Three Apostles. L. W. P. phot.

936. Angoulême, (Charente), Cathédrale. Western façade, northern lunette. Three Apostles. A. K. P. phot.

937. Angoulême, (Charente), Cathédrale. Western façade, lunette north of central portal, detail. An Apostle. Giraudon phot. from cast.

938. ANGOULÊME, (Charente), Cathédrale. Western façade, lunette south of central portal. St. Peter and two Apostles. B.-A. phot.

939. ANGOULÊME, (Charente), Cathédrale. Western façade, lintel of lunette south of central portal. Giraudon phot. from cast.

940. ANGOULÊME, (Charente), Cathédrale. Western façade, southern lunette. Three Apostles. L. W. P. phot.

941. ST.-AMAND-DE-BOIXE, (Charente). Western façade of northern transept, second zone, southern relief. St. Amand. L. W. P. phot.

942. ST.-AMAND-DE-BOIXE, (Charente). Western façade of northern transept, second zone, central relief. L. W. P. phot.

943. ST.-AMAND-DE-BOIXE, (Charente). Western façade of northern transept, second zone, northern relief. L. W. P. phot.

944. ST.-AMAND-DE-BOIXE, (Charente). Western façade of northern transept, northern lunette. Three Apostles. L. W. P. phot.

945. ST.-AMAND-DE-BOIXE, (Charente). Western façade of northern transept, southern lunette. St. Peter and two Apostles. L. W. P. phot.

946. ST.-JOUIN-DE-MARNE, (Deux-Sèvres). Gable. Christ, a Cherub, an Archangel. St. Mary Magdalen (?). F. M. S. phot. from cast.

947. ST.-JOUIN-DE-MARNE, (Deux-Sèvres). Western façade, portion north of central window. Constantine (?), Cain and Abel (?), St. Helena (?), L. W. P. phot.

948. ST.-JOUIN-DE-MARNE, (Deux-Sèvres). Western façade, portion south of central window. Delilah (?), Samson, Annunciation. F. M. S. phot.

949. ST.-JOUIN-DE-MARNE, (Deux-Sèvres). Relief of western façade, south of window, below. St. John. F. M. S. phot. from cast.

950. ST.-JOUIN-DE-MARNE, (Deux-Sèvres). Relief of western façade, south of window, middle. St. Peter. F. M. S. phot. from cast.

951. POITIERS, (Vienne), Notre-Dame-la-Grande. West façade, gable. *Majestas Domini* with the four Evangelists and two Witnesses. L. W. P. phot.

952. POITIERS, (Vienne), Notre-Dame-la-Grande. Western façade, northern half, upper register. St. Peter, an Apostle, St. Hilaire. L. W. P. phot.

953. POITIERS, (Vienne), Norte-Dame-la-Grande. Western façade, upper zone, southern section. St. Martin (?), six Apostles. F. M. S. phot.

954. POITIERS, (Vienne), Notre-Dame-la-Grande. Western façade, middle zone, northern section. Four Apostles. L. W. P. phot.

955. POITIERS, (Vienne), Notre-Dame-la-Grande. Western façade, middle zone, northern section, southern end. Two Apostles. Stoedtner phot.

956. POITIERS, (Vienne), Notre-Dame-la-Grande. Western façade, lower zone, northern end. Temptation; Nebuchadnezzar. L. W. P. phot.

957. POITIERS, (Vienne), Notre-Dame-la-Grande. Western façade, lower zone, northern end. The Temptation. Stoedtner phot.

958. POITIERS, (Vienne), Notre-Dame-la-Grande. Western façade, lower zone, northern arch. Nebuchadnezzar, Daniel, Moses, Jeremiah, Isaiah. L. W. P. phot.

959. POITIERS, (Vienne), Notre-Dame-la-Grande. Western façade, lower zone, northern spandrel. The Annunciation; Jesse. L. W. P. phot.

960. POITIERS, (Vienne), Notre-Dame-la-Grande. Western façade, lower zone, southern spandrel. L. W. P. phot.

961. POITIERS, (Vienne), Notre-Dame-la-Grande. Western façade, lower zone, southern arch. Portions of Nativity and Visitation. L. W. P. phot.

962. POITIERS, (Vienne), Notre-Dame-la-Grande. Western façade, lower zone, southern end. The Nativity. L. W. P. phot.

963. MAILLEZAIS, (Vendée). Detail of northern jamb of western portal. L. W. P. phot.

964. AIRVAULT, (Deux-Sèvres). Altar-frontal. *Majestas Domini;* St. Peter, three Apostles. Stoedtner phot.

965. ANGERS, (Maine-et-Loire), St.-Aubin. Voussure of refectory portal, now in Préfecture. Psychomachia. A. K. P. phot.

966. ANGERS, (Maine-et-Loire), St.-Aubin. Voussure of refectory portal, now in Préfecture. Angel. A. K. P. phot.

967. ANGERS, (Maine-et-Loire), St.-Aubin. Voussure of refectory portal, now in Préfecture. Psychomachia. A. K. P. phot.

968. ANGERS, (Maine-et-Loire), St.-Aubin. Voussure of refectory portal, now in Préfecture. Psychomachia. A. K. P. phot.

969. ANGERS, (Maine-et-Loire), St.-Aubin. Voussure of refectory portal, now in Préfecture. An Angel. L. W. P. phot.

970. ANGERS, (Maine-et-Loire), St.-Aubin. Voussure of refectory portal, now in Préfecture. Moses. L. W. P. phot.

971. ANGERS, (Maine-et-Loire), St.-Aubin. Voussure of refectory portal, now in Préfecture. Psychomachia; an Angel. L. W. P. phot.

972. ANGERS, (Maine-et-Loire), St.-Aubin. Voussure of refectory portal, now in Préfecture. An Angel. L. W. P. phot.

973. CHÂTEAUNEUF-SUR-CHARENTE, (Charente). Voussures of western portal. Lamb of God; Angels. L. W. P. phot.

974. SAINTES, (Charente-Inférieure), Ste.-Marie-des-Dames. Western portal, voussure. Divine Hand, Angels. F. M. S. phot.

975. SAINTES, (Charente-Inférieure), Ste.-Marie-des-Dames. Western portal, middle voussures. F. M. S. phot.

976. SAINTES, (Charente-Inférieure), Ste.-Marie-des-Dames. Western portal, voussures. F. M. S. phot.

977. FONTAINES-D'OZILLAC, (Charente-Inférieure). Western portal, detail of voussures. Psychomachia; Angels. L. W. P. phot.

978. FONTAINES-D'OZILLAC, (Charente-Inférieure). Western portal, detail of voussures. An Angel. L. W. P. phot.

979. AULNAY, (Charente-Inférieure), St.-Pierre. Southern transept, portal. Grotesques, Elders, Saints. L. W. P. phot.

980. AULNAY, (Charente-Inférieure). Window of southern transept, detail of voussure. Psychomachia. Stoedtner phot.

981. AULNAY, (Charente-Inférieure). Eastern window, detail of jamb. F. M. S. phot.

982. AULNAY, (Charente-Inférieure). Capital of nave. Cain and Abel. B.-A. phot.

983. AULNAY, (Charente-Inférieure). Western façade, northern lunette. Crucifixion of St. Peter. L. W. P. phot.

984. AULNAY, (Charente-Inférieure). Western portal. Zodiac, wise and foolish Virgins; Psychomachia; Angels. L. W. P. phot.

985. AULNAY, (Charente-Inférieure), St.-Pierre. Western portal, detail of voussures. Foolish Virgins, Psychomachia. L. W. P. phot.

986. AULNAY, (Charente-Inférieure), St.-Pierre. Western façade, southern lunette. Christ, the Virgin and St. John. L. W. P. phot.

987. ARGENTON-CHÂTEAU, (Deux-Sèvres). Western portal, northern spandrel. The Feast of Dives, Zodiac. L. W. P. phot.

988. ARGENTON-CHÂTEAU, (Deux-Sèvres). Western portal, southern spandrel. Lazarus and Dives; Zodiac; Apostles. L. W. P. phot.

989. ARGENTON-CHÂTEAU, (Deux-Sèvres). Western portal, detail of voussures. Christ; wise and foolish Virgins; Humility, Faith. L. W. P. phot.

990. ARGENTON-CHÂTEAU, (Deux-Sèvres). Western portal, detail of voussures. St. John, a wise Virgin. L. W. P. phot.

991. ARGENTON-CHÂTEAU, (Deux-Sèvres). Western portal, detail of voussures. Chastity and Luxury. L. W. P. phot.

992. ARGENTON-CHÂTEAU, (Deux-Sèvres). Western portal, detail of voussures. St. Thomas. L. W. P. phot.

993. ARGENTON-CHÂTEAU, (Deux-Sèvres). Western portal, northern voussures. Zodiac, Apostles, wise Virgins. A. K. P. phot.

994. ARGENTON-CHÂTEAU, (Deux-Sèvres). Western portal, detail of voussures. An Angel. L. W. P. phot.

995. ARGENTON-CHÂTEAU, (Deux-Sèvres). Western portal, detail of voussures. August, Libra; St. Paul, St. James, St. Bartholomew. L. W. P. phot.

996. ARGENTON-CHÂTEAU, (Deux-Sèvres). Western portal, detail of voussures. St. Bartholomew; an Apostle; foolish Virgins. L. W. P. phot.

997. FENIOUX, (Charente-Inférieure). Western façade. Christ, six Apostles; Zodiac; wise and foolish Virgins; Angels; Psychomachia. L. W. P. phot.

998. FENIOUX, (Charente-Inférieure). Western portal, detail of northern voussures. An Angel; Psychomachia. L. W. P. phot.

999. VARAIZE, (Charente-Inférieure). Voussures of the southern portal. Angels, Psychomachia. A. K. P. phot.

1000. VARAIZE, (Charente-Inférieure). Voussures of southern portal. Angels, Psychomachia. A. K. P. phot.

1001. VARAIZE, (Charente-Inférieure). Voussures of southern portal. An Angel, Elders (?). L. W. P. phot.

1002. VARAIZE, (Charente-Inférieure). Voussures of southern portal. An Angel; Elders (?). L. W. P. phot.

1003. PONT-L'ABBÉ-D'ARNOULT, (Charente-Inférieure). Western façade, northern lunette. L. W. P. phot.

1004. PONT-L'ABBÉ-D'ARNOULT, (Charente-Inférieure). Western façade, central tympanum. Wise and foolish Virgins; St. Catherine and other Saints; Psychomachia; Angels. L. W. P. phot.

1005. PONT-L'ABBÉ-D'ARNOULT, (Charente-Inférieure). Western façade, southern lunette. Crucifixion of St. Peter. L. W. P. phot.

1006. ST.-MICHEL, (Charente). Tympanum of portal. St. Michael and the Dragon. L. W. P. phot.

1007. ST.-SYMPHORIEN, (Charente-Inférieure). Western façade, upper register. Psychomachia. L. W. P. phot.

1008. CHÂTEAUNEUF-SUR-CHARENTE, (Charente). Western façade, upper zone, northern lunette. Constantine and St. Helena. L. W. P. phot.

1009. CHÂTEAUNEUF-SUR-CHARENTE, (Charente). Western façade, relief north of central window. St. Peter. L. W. P. phot.

1010. CHÂTEAUNEUF-SUR-CHARENTE, (Charente). Western façade, upper zone, reliefs south of central window. A Sibyl (?) and a Prophet. L. W. P. phot.

1011. MELLE, (Deux-Sèvres), St.-Hilaire. Northern portal. Constantine, fragments of Psychomachia and Zodiac. B.-A. phot.

1012. CORME-ROYAL, (Charente-Inférieure). Western façade, upper zone. St. Michael; Saints; wise and foolish Virgins; Psychomachia. L. W. P. phot.

1013. CORME-ROYAL, (Charente-Inférieure). Western façade, upper zone, northern lunette. St. Catherine, other Saints. L. W. P. phot.

1014. CORME-ROYAL, (Charente-Inférieure). Detail of voussure, central arch, upper story. The Foolish Virgins. L. W. P. phot.

1015. CORME-ROYAL, (Charente-Inférieure). Western façade, upper zone, southern lunette. Psychomachia. L. W. P. phot.

1016. CORME-ROYAL, (Charente-Inférieure). Western façade, lower part. Donors(?); Ecclesiastics; Angels; Saints (?). L. W. P. phot.

1017. CORME-ROYAL, (Charente-Inférieure). Voussures of central portal. Ecclesiastics, Angels. L. W. P. phot.

1018. PÉRIGNAC, (Charente-Inférieure). Western façade, upper zone. *Majestas Domini*. L. W. P. phot.

1019. PÉRIGNAC, (Charente-Inférieure). Western façade, upper gallery, northern portion. Psychomachia. L. W. P. phot.

1020. PÉRIGNAC, (Charente-Inférieure). Western façade, upper gallery south of window. Psychomachia. L. W. P. phot.

1021. Pérignac, (Charente-Inférieure). Western façade, southern half, upper gallery. Psychomachia. L. W. P phot.

1022. Pérignac, (Charente-Inférieure). Western façade, lower gallery, northern portion. St. Peter, three Apostles. L. W. P. phot.

1023. Pérignac, (Charente-Inférieure). Western façade, lower gallery, central portion. Christ, two Apostles. L. W. P. phot.

1024. Pérignac, (Charente-Inférieure). Western façade, lower gallery, southern portion. Four Apostles. L. W. P. phot.

1025. Ruffec, (Charente). Western façade, upper zone. The Ascension. L. W. P. phot.

1026. Ruffec, (Charente). Western façade, middle zone, northern portion. Detail of the Ascension; four Apostles. L. W. P. phot.

1027. Ruffec, (Charente). Western façade, middle zone, north of window. Detail of the Ascension; St. Peter. L. W. P. phot.

1028. Ruffec, (Charente). Western façade, middle zone, south of window. Detail of the Ascension; two Apostles. L. W. P. phot.

1029. Ruffec, (Charente). Western façade, northern lunette. Samson and Delilah. L. W. P. phot.

1030. Montmorillon, (Vienne). Octagone. Sculptures of façade. Luxury; other subjects. L. W. P. phot.

1031. Matha, (Charente-Inférieure). Western façade, northern half, upper part. Constantine. L. W. P. phot.

1032. Matha, (Charente-Inférieure). Statue of façade, with head from elsewhere. L. W. P. phot.

1033. Matha, (Charente-Inférieure). Statue of façade, with head from elsewhere. L. W. P. phot.

1034. Chadennac, (Charente-Inférieure). Western portal. 1140. L. W. P. phot.

1035. Chadennac, (Charente-Inférieure). Western portal, voussures. 1140. L. W. P. phot.

1036. Chadennac, (Charente-Inférieure). Western portal, voussures. 1140. L. W. P. phot.

1037. Chadennac, (Charente-Inférieure). Western façade, northern lunette. Noble Donors (?), St. Hilaire (?). 1140. B.-A. phot.

1038. Chadennac, (Charente-Inférieure). Western façade, northern spandrel. A Donor (?). 1140. L. W. P. phot.

1039. Chadennac, (Charente-Inférieure). Western façade, southern spandrel. St. Michael. 1140. L. W. P. phot.

1040. Chadennac, (Charente-Inférieure). Western façade, southern end. St. Michael, St. Martin (?). 1140. L. W. P. phot.

1041. Blazimont, (Gironde). Western portal, voussure. Psychomachia. L. W. P. phot.

1042. Blazimont, (Gironde). Western portal, voussure. Psychomachia. L. W. P. phot.

1043. BLAZIMONT, (Gironde). Western portal, voussure. An Angel. L. W. P. phot.

1044. BLAZIMONT, (Gironde). Western portal, detail of voussures. Psychomachia. L. W. P. phot.

1045. PARTHENAY, (Deux-Sèvres), Notre-Dame-de-la-Couldre. Capital now in gate of adjoining school. David and Goliath. L. W. P. phot.

1046. PARTHENAY, (Deux-Sèvres), Notre-Dame-de-la-Couldre. Capital now in gate of adjoining school. The Sacrifice of Abraham. L. W. P. phot.

1047. PARTHENAY, (Deux-Sèvres), Notre-Dame-de-la-Couldre. Central portal, northern capital. L. W. P. phot.

1048. PARTHENAY, (Deux-Sèvres), Notre-Dame-de-la-Couldre. Western portal, northern voussures. An Elder, Psychomachia, the Annunciation; the Virgin. L. W. P. phot.

1049. PARTHENAY, (Deux-Sèvres), Notre-Dame-de-la-Couldre. Western portal, voussures. Angels. L. W. P. phot.

1050. PARTHENAY, (Deux-Sèvres), Notre-Dame-de-la-Couldre. Western portal, voussures. Psychomachia, Angels. L. W. P. phot.

1051. PARTHENAY, (Deux-Sèvres), Notre-Dame-de-la-Couldre. Western portal, southern voussures. Elder, Psychomachia, Annunciation to Zacharias. L. W. P. phot.

1052. PARTHENAY, (Deux-Sèvres), Notre-Dame-de-la-Couldre. Western façade, northern lunette. Constantine. A. K. P. phot.

1053. PARTHENAY, (Deux-Sèvres), Notre-Dame-de-la-Couldre. Fragment of frieze of western façade, now in Louvre. The Shepherds. From Sadoux' engraving, made before the restoration.

1054. PARTHENAY, (Deux-Sèvres), Notre-Dame-de-la-Couldre. Fragment of frieze of western façade, now in Louvre. The Shepherds. Restored. F. M. S. phot.

1055. PARTHENAY, (Deux-Sèvres), Notre-Dame-de-la-Couldre. Reliefs from western façade, now in Louvre. An Elder. From Sadoux' engraving.

1056. PARTHENAY, (Deux-Sèvres), Notre-Dame-de-la-Couldre. Relief from western façade, now in Louvre. An Elder. From Sadoux' engraving.

1057. PARTHENAY, (Deux-Sèvres), Notre-Dame-de-la-Couldre. Reliefs from western façade, now in Louvre. Two Elders. Giraudon phot.

1058. ST.-POMPAIN, (Deux-Sèvres). Voussures of western portal. Psychomachia. Signed by Gilglelm. L. W. P. phot.

1059. THOUARS, (Deux-Sèvres), St.-Médard. Western façade. *Majestas Domini;* Apostles; Angels, Prophets, Saints, Entry into Jerusalem. Restored. L. W. P. phot.

1060. THOUARS, (Deux-Sèvres), St.-Médard. Western façade, detail. *Majestas Domini.* Restored. L. W. P. phot.

1061. FOUSSAIS, (Vendée). Western façade, northern lunette. Deposition. Signed by Giraud Audebert of St.-Jean-d'Angély. L. W. P. phot.

1062. FOUSSAIS, (Vendée). Western façade, central portal. L. W. P. phot.

1063. FOUSSAIS, (Vendée). Western façade, southern lunette. *Noli me tangere.* Feast at the House of Simon. L. W. P. phot.

1064. TROIS-PALIS, (Charente). Gable of western façade. *Majestas Domini.* L. W. P. phot.

1065. MOREAUX, (Vienne). Portion of western façade with relief of a Bishop. *c.* 1140. A. K. P. phot.

1066. MOREAUX, (Vienne). Western portal, southern jamb. *c.* 1140. A. K. P. phot.

1067. MOREAUX, (Vienne). Relief north of western portal. A Bishop. *c.* 1140. L. W. P. phot.

1068. MOREAUX, (Vienne). Western façade, relief south of portal. A Bishop. L. W. P. phot.

1069. ANGERS (Maine-et-Loire), St.-Aubin. Voussures of cloister, now in Préfecture. David and Goliath. L. W. P. phot.

1070. ANGERS, (Maine-et-Loire), St.-Aubin. Arch of cloister, now in Préfecture. Angels, Virgin. Giraudon phot.

1071. ST.-SATURNIN, (Charente). Lunette of façade. Two Saints. L. W. P. phot.

1072. ST.-SATURNIN, (Charente). Lunette of façade. Christ and two Apostles. L. W. P. phot.

1072 a. MONTMORILLON, (Vienne), Eglise du Seminaire. Western façade, frieze. Annunciation, Nativity, Shepherds. L. W. P. phot.

1073. MONTMORILLON, (Vienne), Eglise du Seminaire. Western façade, frieze. Shepherds, Presentation, Adoration, Flight. L. W. P. phot.

1074. SELLES-SUR-CHER, (Loire-et-Cher). Sculptures in exterior of apse. L. W. P. phot.

1075. SELLES-SUR-CHER, (Loire-et-Cher). Relief of apse. St. Michael. L. W. P. phot.

1076. SELLES-SUR-CHER, (Loire-et-Cher). Relief in north wall of choir. The Visitation. A. K. P. phot.

1077. SELLES-SUR-CHER, (Loire-et-Cher). Apse, detail of lower frieze. The Nativity. A. K. P. phot.

1078. SELLES-SUR-CHER, (Loire-et-Cher). Apse, detail of lower frieze. The Resurrection of Lazarus. L. W. P. phot.

1079. SELLES-SUR-CHER, (Loire-et-Cher). Apse, detail of lower frieze. The Last Supper; Washing the Feet. B.-A. phot.

1080. SELLES-SUR-CHER, (Loire-et-Cher). Apse, detail of lower frieze. The Betrayal. L. W. P. phot.

1081. SELLES-SUR-CHER, (Loire-et-Cher). Apse, detail of lower frieze. Christ before Pilate. L. W. P. phot.

1082. SELLES-SUR-CHER, (Loire-et-Cher). Exterior of apse, detail of upper frieze. St. Eustice's Sheep guarded by Wolves; the Miracle of the Bread. B.-A. phot.

1083. Villogen, (Charente). Relief south of western portal. Fall of the rebellious Angels. L. W. P. phot.

1084. Villogen, (Charente). Relief north of western portal. L. W. P. phot.

1085. St.-Vivien, (Gironde). Lunette of apse. L. W. P. phot.

1086. St.-Vivien, (Gironde). Lunette of apse. L. W. P. phot.

1087. Chalais, (Charente). Western façade. Prophets (?), three Saints (?); the Maries at the Tomb. L. W. P. phot.

1088. Chalais, (Charente). Western façade, northern lunette. Three Saints (?). L. W. P. phot.

1089. Chalais, (Charente). Western façade, southern lunette. The Maries at the Tomb. L. W. P. phot.

1090. Melle, (Deux-Sèvres). St.-Pierre. Relief over southern portal. Christ, St. Peter and St. Paul. L. W. P. phot.

1091. Melle, (Deux-Sèvres). St.-Pierre. Capital of nave. Entombment of St. Hilaire. L. W. P. phot.

1092. Surgères, (Charente-Inférieure). Western façade, northern upper lunette. A Horseman. L. W. P. phot.

1093. Surgères, (Charente-Inférieure). Western façade, southern upper lunette. Constantine. L. W. P. phot.

1093a. Caen, (Calvados), St.-Etienne-le-Vieux. Relief in exterior of choir. Constantine (?).

1094. Gensac-la-Pallue, (Charente). Relief of western façade. The Virgin. L. W. P. phot.

1095. Gensac-la-Pallue, (Charente). Relief of western façade. St. Ausone. L. W. P. phot.

1096. Cognac, (Charente). Detail of voussures, western portal. July, August, September. L. W. P. phot.

1097. Aubeterre, (Charente), St.-Jacques. Western façade, detail of upper northern portion. Constantine. L. W. P. phot.

1098. Aubeterre, (Charente), St.-Jacques. Western façade, northern lunette, frieze. May, April, March, February. L. W. P. phot.

1099. Aubeterre, (Charente), St.-Jacques. Western façade, northern lunette, frieze. February, January, December. L. W. P. phot.

1100. L'Ile-Bouchard, (Indre-et-Loire), St.-Léonard. Capital of ambulatory. The Baptism; Slaughter of the Innocents. L. W. P. phot.

1101. L'Ile-Bouchard, (Indre-et-Loire), St.-Léonard. Capital of ambulatory. The Annunciation; the Visitation. L. W. P. phot.

1102. L'Ile-Bouchard, (Indre-et-Loire), St.-Léonard. Capital of ambulatory. Presentation. B.-A. phot.

1103. L'Ile-Bouchard, (Indre-et-Loire), St.-Léonard. Capital of ambulatory. The Entry into Jerusalem; the Temptation. L. W. P. phot.

1104. L'Ile-Bouchard, (Indre-et-Loire), St.-Léonard. Capital of ambulatory. The Last Supper. L. W. P. phot.

WESTERN FRANCE

1105. L'ILE-BOUCHARD, (Indre-et-Loire), St.-Léonard. Capital of ambulatory. Last Supper, Betrayal. B.-A. phot.

1106. L'ILE-BOUCHARD, (Indre-et-Loire), St.-Léonard. Capital of ambulatory. The Temptation. L. W. P. phot.

1107. L'ILE-BOUCHARD, (Indre-et-Loire), St.-Léonard. Capital of ambulatory. The Crucifixion, the Last Supper. L. W. P. phot.

1108. LOCHES, (Indre-et-Loire), St.-Ours. Console in choir. L. W. P. phot.

1109. LOCHES, (Indre-et-Loire), St.-Ours. Console in choir. A. K. P. phot.

1110. LOCHES, (Indre-et-Loire), St.-Ours. Console in choir. A. K. P. phot.

1111. LOCHES, (Indre-et-Loire), St.-Ours. Western portal. Adoration of the Magi; St. Ours (?), St. Peter, the Liberal Arts. L. W. P. phot.

1112. LOCHES, (Indre-et-Loire), St.-Ours. Western portal, upper zone, northern portion. Adoration of the Magi. L. W. P. phot.

1113. LOCHES, (Indre-et-Loire), St.-Ours. Relief over western portal. Detail of the Adoration of the Magi. The Virgin and St. Joseph. L. W. P. phot.

1114. LOCHES, (Indre-et-Loire), St.-Ours. Western portal, upper zone, southern portion. St. Joseph, the Magi. L. W. P. phot.

1115. LOCHES, (Indre-et-Loire), St.-Ours. Sculptured colonnettes embedded in western portal, middle zone, northern side. L. W. P. phot.

1116. LOCHES, (Indre-et-Loire), St.-Ours. Western portal, detail of voussures. Philosophy, Grammar. L. W. P. phot.

1117. LOCHES, (Indre-et-Loire), St.-Ours. Sculptured colonnettes embedded in western portal, middle zone, southern side. L. W. P. phot.

1118. LOCHES, (Indre-et-Loire), St.-Ours. Western portal, northern jamb. St. Ours. L. W. P. phot.

1119. LOCHES, (Indre-et-Loire), St.-Ours. Western portal, southern jamb. St. Peter. L. W. P. phot.

1120. LA VILLEDIEU, (Vienne). Relief of western façade. A Prophet. L. W. P. phot.

1121. LA VILLEDIEU, (Vienne). Relief of western façade. The Annunciation. L. W. P. phot.

1122. CIVRAY, (Vienne), St.-Nicolas. Western façade, second story, northern spandrel. Two Prophets, Angels, Psychomachia. L. W. P. phot.

1123. CIVRAY, (Vienne), St.-Nicolas. Western façade, second story, northern spandrel. Two Prophets, Angels, Psychomachia. L. W. P. phot.

1124. CIVRAY, (Vienne), St.-Nicolas. Western façade, second story, central window. Psychomachia, St. Paul, St. Peter. L. W. P. phot.

1125. CIVRAY, (Vienne), St.-Nicolas. Western façade, second story, southern spandrel. Two Prophets, Psychomachia, Prophets. L. W. P. phot.

1126. CIVRAY, (Vienne), St.-Nicolas. Western façade, second zone, northern lunette. Constantine. L. W. P. phot.

1127. CIVRAY, (Vienne), St.-Nicolas. Western façade, second story, southern lunette. Prophets. L. W. P. phot.

1128. CIVRAY, (Vienne), St.-Nicolas. Western façade, upper zone, southern lunette, lower portion. The Church, St. Nicolas and the three dowerless Maidens (?). L. W. P. phot.

1129. CIVRAY, (Vienne), St.-Nicolas. Western façade, upper zone, southern lunette, lower portion. Three dowerless Maidens and their Father (?), the Synagogue. L. W. P. phot.

1130. CIVRAY, (Vienne), St.-Nicolas. Western portal, voussures. Virgin, Angels, Christ, wise Virgins. L. W. P. phot.

1131. CIVRAY, (Vienne), St.-Nicolas. Western façade, central portal, voussures. Angel, foolish Virgins. L. W. P. phot.

1132. POITIERS, (Vienne), Musée des Antiquaires de l'Ouest. Fragment said to come from St.-Benoît. Four Apostles. L. W. P. phot.

1133. POITIERS, (Vienne), Musée des Antiquaires de l'Ouest. Fragment said to come from St.-Benoît. Three Apostles. L. W. P. phot.

1134. POITIERS, (Vienne), St.-Hilaire-la-Celle. "Tombeau de St. Hilaire." Death of the Saint. F. M. S. phot. from cast.

1135. ST.-AMAND-DE-BOIXE, (Charente-Inférieure). Western portal, detail. F. M. S. phot.

1136. VOUVANT, (Vendée). Façade of north transept. The Last Supper; Samson and Delilah, Samson and the Lion. L. W. P. phot.

1137. CROUZILLES, (Indre-et-Loire). Statue of façade. Restored. L. W. P. phot.

1138. CROUZILLES, (Indre-et-Loire). Statue of façade. L. W. P. phot.

896. Azay-le-Rideau, (Indre-et-Loire). Reliefs in western façade. Christ and twelve Apostles. L. W. P. phot.

897. CHINON, (Indre-et-Loire), St.-Mesme. Relief in ancient façade. The Crucifixion. L. W. P. phot. from a cast.

898. AIRVAULT, (Deux-Sèvres). Spandrel of nave arcade. F. M. S. phot.

899.   AIRVAULT, (Deux-Sèvres).   Spandrel of nave arcade.   B. A. phot.

900. AIRVAULT, (Deux-Sèvres). Clerestory wall and vaulting capital. Feast at Emmaus; two Saints. F. M. S. phot.

901. Airvault, (Deux-Sèvres). Capital of nave. Temptation; Adam and Eve
reproved. F. M. S. phot.

902.   AIRVAULT, (Deux-Sèvres).   Capital of nave.   F. M. S. phot.

903. AIRVAULT, (Deux-Sèvres). Tomb of the abbot Pierre de Saine-Fontaine, † 1110. L. W. P. phot.

904. CHAUVIGNY, (Vienne), St.-Pierre. Capital of ambulatory. Babylon; the Shepherds. Stoedtner phot.

905. CHAUVIGNY, (Vienne), St.-Pierre. Capital of ambulatory. Adoration of the Magi. Signed by Joffre. A. K. P. phot.

906. SAINTES, (Charente-Inférieure), Musée Archéologique. Capital. Three
Apostles, St. Luke. A. K. P. phot.

907 POITIERS, (Vienne), Ste.-Radegonde. Relief now in vestibule. Christ.
L. W. P. phot.

908. POITIERS, (Vienne), Ste.-Radegonde. Relief now in vestibule. Ste.-Rade-
gonde. L. W. P. phot.

909. POITIERS, (Vienne), Ste.-Radegonde. Capital of ambulatory. Daniel and Habakkuk. F. M. S. phot.

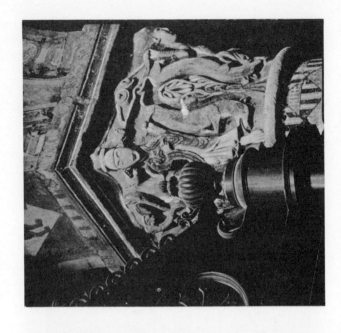

910. POITIERS, (Vienne), Ste.-Radegonde. Capital of ambulatory. God, Adam and Eve. F. M. S. phot.

911. POITIERS, (Vienne), Ste.-Radegonde. Capital of ambulatory. F. M. S. phot.

912. POITIERS, (Vienne), St.-Hilaire. Relief in transept gable. F. M. S. phot. from cast.

913. POITIERS, (Vienne), St.-Hilaire. Capital now in Musée des Antiquaires de l'Ouest. F. M. S. phot.

914. POITIERS, (Vienne), St.-Hilaire. Relief in transept gable. F. M. S. phot. from cast.

915. POITIERS, (Vienne), St.-Hilaire. Capital. Death of St. Hilaire. F. M. S. phot. from cast.

918. Saintes, (Charente-Inférieure), St.-Eutrope. Capital of nave. Psychostasy. B.-A. phot.

919. St.-Symphorien, (Charente-Inférieure). Western façade, portal. L. W. P. phot.

920.   BORDEAUX, (Gironde), Ste.-Croix. Western portal, voussure. Angels, Elders.
L. W. P. phot.

921. BORDEAUX, (Gironde), Ste.-Croix. Western façade, southern lunette. Five Representations of the Vice of Luxury. L. W. P. phot.

922. ANGERS, (Maine-et-Loire), Eglise du Ronceray. Capital in Musée Archéologique. Entry into Jerusalem. L. W. P. phot

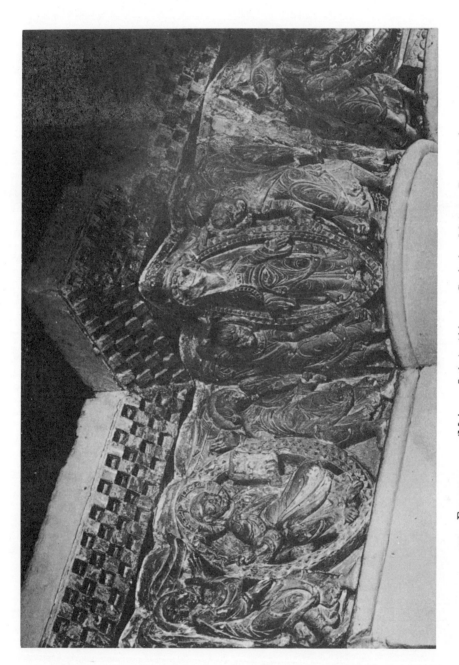

923. Fontevrault, (Maine-et-Loire), Abbaye. Capital. *Majestas Domini*; the Assumption. B.-A. phot.

924. PARTHENAY-LE-VIEUX, (Deux-Sèvres). Western façade, northern lunette. Constantine. L. W. P. phot.

925. PARTHENAY-LE-VIEUX, (Deux-Sèvres). Western façade, southern lunette.
Samson. L. W. P. phot.

926. CASTELVIEIL, (Gironde). Southern portal, detail of voussures. L. W. P. phot.

927. Castelvieil, (Gironde). Southern portal, detail of voussures. Psychomachia. L. W. P. phot.

928. Castelvieil, (Gironde). Southern portal, detail. L. W. P. phot.

929. ANGOULÊME, (Charente), Cathédrale. Western façade, central portion, upper zone. *Majestas Domini*, Angels, Saints. L. W. P. phot.

930. ANGOULÊME, (Charente), Cathédrale. Western façade, central portion, fifth zone. St. Mark, St. Luke, Saints, Angels. L. W. P. phot.

931.   ANGOULÊME, (Charente), Cathédrale.   Western façade, southern half, fourth and fifth zones.   Prophets, Apostles, Vices (?).   B.-A. phot

932. Angoulême, (Charente), Cathédrale. Western façade, northern half, fourth and fifth zones. Prophets, Vices (?), an Apostle, St. Peter. B.-A. phot.

933. Angoulême, (Charente), Cathédrale. Western façade, northern side, fourth zone. St. Peter, an Apostle. Stoedtner phot.

934. ANGOULÊME, (Charente), Cathédrale. Western façade, northern portion, third zone. Three Apostles. L. W. P. phot.

935. ANGOULÊME, (Charente), Cathédrale. Western façade, southern side, third zone. Three Apostles. L. W. P. phot.

936. ANGOULÊME, (Charente), Cathédrale. Western façade, northern lunette. Three Apostles. A. K. P. phot.

937. ANGOULÊME, (Charente), Cathédrale. Western façade, lunette north of
central portal, detail. An Apostle. Giraudon phot. from cast.

938. ANGOULÊME, (Charente), Cathédrale. Western façade, lunette south of central portal. St. Peter and two Apostles. B.-A. phot.

939. ANGOULÊME, (Charente), Cathédrale. Western façade, lintel of lunette south of central portal. Giraudon phot. from cast.

940. Angoulême, (Charente), Cathédrale. Western façade, southern lunette. Three Apostles. L. W. P. phot.

941. St.-Amand-de-Boixe, (Charente). Western façade of northern transept, second zone, southern relief. St. Amand. L. W. P. phot.

942. St.-Amand-de-Boixe, (Charente). Western façade of northern transept, second zone, central relief. L. W. P. phot.

943. St.-Amand-de-Boixe, (Charente). Western façade of northern transept, second zone, northern relief. L. W. P. phot.

944. St.-Amand-de-Boixe, (Charente). Western façade of northern transept, northern lunette. Three Apostles. L. W. P. phot.

945. St.-Amand-de-Boixe, (Charente). Western façade of northern transept, southern lunette. St. Peter and two Apostles. L. W. P. phot.

946.   ST.-JOUIN-DE-MARNE, (Deux-Sèvres). Gable. Christ, a Cherub, an Archangel.
St. Mary Magdalen (?). F. M. S. phot. from cast.

947. St.-Jouin-de-Marne, (Deux-Sèvres). Western façade, portion north of central window. Constantine (?), Cain and Abel (?), St. Helena (?), L. W. P. phot.

948. St.-Jouin-de-Marne, (Deux-Sèvres). Western façade, portion south of central window. Delilah (?), Samson, Annunciation. F. M. S. phot.

949. St.-Jouin-de-Marne, (Deux-Sèvres). Relief of western façade, south of window, below. St. John. F. M. S. phot. from cast.

950. St.-Jouin-de-Marne, (Deux-Sèvres). Relief of western façade, south of window, middle. St. Peter. F. M. S. phot. from cast.

951. Poitiers, (Vienne), Notre-Dame-la-Grande. West façade, gable. *Majestas Domini* with the four Evangelists and two Witnesses. L. W. P. phot.

952. POITIERS, (Vienne), Notre-Dame-la-Grande. Western façade, northern half, upper register. St. Peter, an Apostle, St. Hilaire. L. W. P. phot.

953. POITIERS, (Vienne), Norte-Dame-la-Grande. Western façade, upper zone, southern section. St. Martin (?), six Apostles. F. M. S. phot.

954. POITIERS, (Vienne), Notre-Dame-la-Grande. Western façade, middle zone, northern section. Four Apostles. L. W. P. phot.

955. POITIERS, (Vienne), Notre-Dame-la-Grande. Western façade, middle zone, northern section southern end. Two Apostles. Stoedtner phot.

956. POITIERS, (Vienne), Notre-Dame-la-Grande.   Western façade, lower zone, northern end. Temptation; Nebuchadnezzar. L. W. P. phot.

957. POITIERS, (Vienne), Notre-Dame-la-Grande. Western façade, lower zone, northern end. The Temptation. Stoedtner phot.

958. POITIERS, (Vienne), Notre-Dame-la-Grande. Western façade, lower zone,
       northern arch. Nebuchadnezzar, Daniel, Moses, Jeremiah, Isaiah.
       L. W. P. phot.

959. POITIERS, (Vienne), Notre-Dame-la-Grande. Western façade, lower zone, northern spandrel. The Annunciation; Jesse. L. W. P. phot.

960. POITIERS, (Vienne), Notre-Dame-la-Grande. Western façade, lower zone,
southern spandrel. L. W. P. phot.

961. POITIERS, (Vienne), Notre-Dame-la-Grande. Western façade, lower zone, southern arch. Portions of Nativity and Visitation. L. W. P. phot.

962. POITIERS, (Vienne), Notre-Dame-la-Grande. Western façade, lower zone, southern end. The Nativity. L. W. P. phot.

963. MAILLEZAIS, (Vendée). Detail of northern jamb of western portal. L. W. P.
phot.

964. AIRVAULT, (Deux-Sèvres). Altar-frontal. *Majestas Domini*; St. Peter, three Apostles. Stoedtner phot.

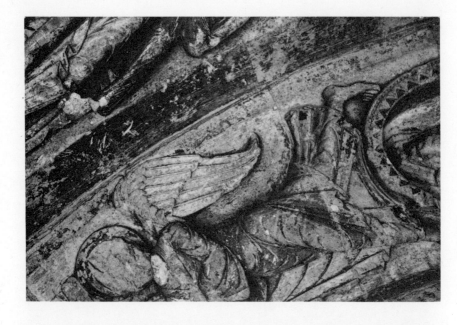

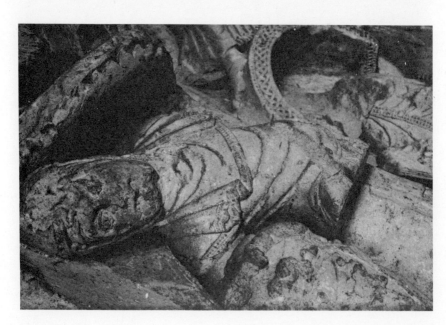

965. ANGERS, (Maine-et-Loire), St.-Aubin. Voussure of refectory portal, now in Préfecture. Psychomachia. A. K. P. phot.

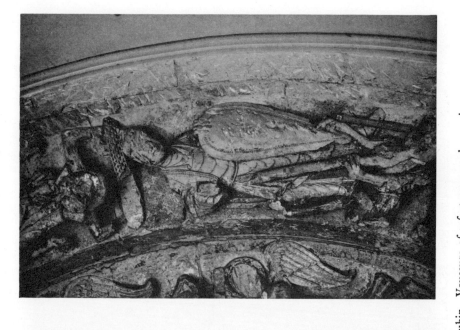

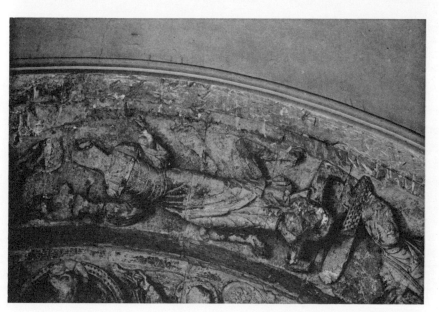

967. ANGERS, (Maine-et-Loire), St.-Aubin. Voussure of refectory portal, now in Préfecture. Psychomachia. A. K. P. phot.

968. ANGERS, (Maine-et-Loire), St.-Aubin. Voussure of refectory portal, now in Préfecture. Psychomachia. A. K. P. phot.

969.   ANGERS, (Maine-et-Loire), St.-Aubin. Voussure of refectory portal, now in
Préfecture. An Angel. L. W. P. phot.

970. ANGERS, (Maine-et-Loire), St.-Aubin. Voussure of refectory portal, now in
Préfecture. Moses. L. W. P. phot.

971. ANGERS, (Maine-et-Loire), St.-Aubin. Voussure of refectory portal, now in
Préfecture. Psychomachia; an Angel. L. W. P. phot.

972. ANGERS, (Maine-et-Loire), St.-Aubin. Voussure of refectory portal, now in Préfecture. An Angel. L. W. P. phot.

973. CHÂTEAUNEUF-SUR-CHARENTE, (Charente). Voussures of western portal. Lamb of God; Angels. L. W. P. phot.

974. SAINTES, (Charente-Inférieure), Ste.-Marie-des-Dames. Western portal, voussure. Divine Hand, Angels. F. M. S. phot.

975. SAINTES, (Charente-Inférieure), Ste.-Marie-des-Dames. Western portal, middle voussures. F. M. S. phot.

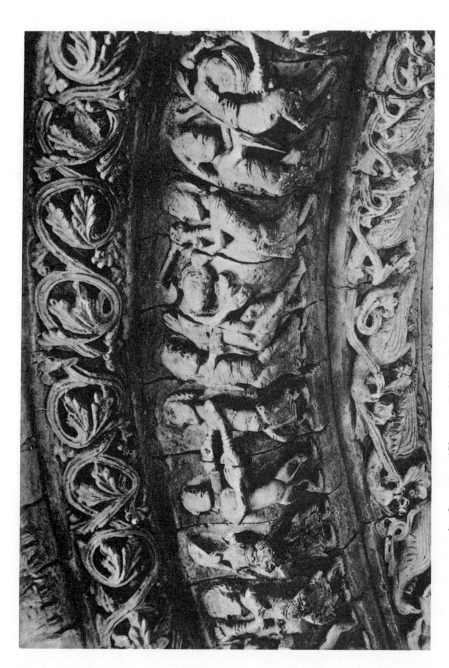

976. SAINTES, (Charente-Inférieure), Ste.-Marie-des-Dames. Western portal, voussures. F. M. S. phot.

977. FONTAINES-D'OZILLAC, (Charente-Inférieure). Western portal, detail of voussures. Psychomachia; Angels. L. W. P. phot.

978. Fontaines-d'Ozillac, (Charente-Inférieure). Western portal, detail of voussures. An Angel. L. W. P. phot.

979. AULNAY, (Charente-Inférieure), St.-Pierre. Southern transept, portal. Grotesques, Elders, Saints. L. W. P. phot.

980. AULNAY, (Charente-Inférieure). Window of southern transept, detail of
voussure. Psychomachia. Stoedtner phot.

981. AULNAY, (Charente-Inférieure). Eastern window, detail of jamb. F. M. S.
phot.

982. AULNAY, (Charente-Inférieure). Capital of nave. Cain and Abel. B.-A. phot.

983. AULNAY, (Charente-Inférieure). Western façade, northern lunette. Crucifixion of St. Peter. L. W. P. phot.

984. AULNAY, (Charente-Inférieure). Western portal. Zodiac, wise and foolish Virgins; Psychomachia; Angels. L. W. P. phot.

985. Aulnay, (Charente-Inférieure), St.-Pierre. Western portal, detail of voussures. Foolish Virgins, Psychomachia. L. W. P. phot.

986. AULNAY, (Charente-Inférieure), St.-Pierre. Western façade, southern lunette. Christ, the Virgin and St. John. L. W. P. phot.

987. ARGENTON-CHÂTEAU, (Deux-Sèvres). Western portal, northern spandrel.
The Feast of Dives. Zodiac. I. W. P. phot.

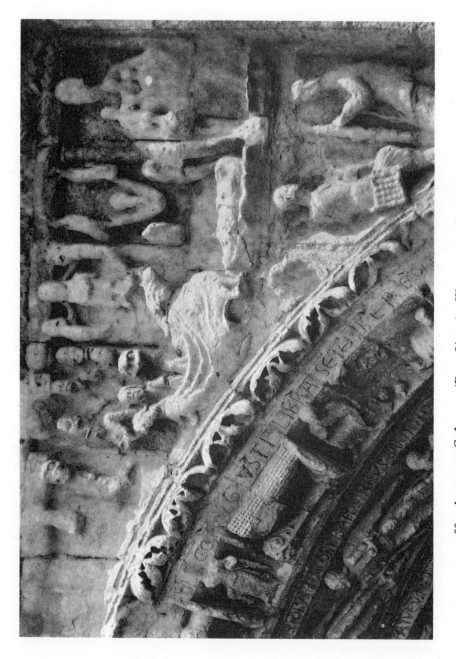

988. ARGENTON-CHÂTEAU, (Deux-Sèvres). Western portal, southern spandrel. Lazarus and Dives; Zodiac; Apostles. L. W. P. phot.

989.   ARGENTON-CHÂTEAU, (Deux-Sèvres).   Western portal, detail of voussures.
Christ; wise and foolish Virgins; Humility, Faith. L. W. P. phot.

990. ARGENTON-CHÂTEAU, (Deux-Sèvres). Western portal, detail of voussures. St. John, a wise Virgin. L. W. P. phot.

991. ARGENTON-CHÂTEAU, (Deux-Sèvres). Western portal, detail of voussures. Chastity and Luxury. L. W. P. phot.

992. ARGENTON-CHÂTEAU, (Deux-Sèvres). Western portal, detail of voussures. St. Thomas. L. W. P. phot.

993. ARGENTON-CHÂTEAU, (Deux-Sèvres). Western portal, northern voussures. Zodiac. Apostles, wise Virgins. A. K. P. phot.

994. ARGENTON-CHÂTEAU, (Deux-Sèvres). Western portal, detail of voussures. An Angel. L. W. P. phot.

995. ARGENTON-CHÂTEAU, (Deux-Sèvres). Western portal, detail of voussures.
August, Libra; St. Paul, St. James, St. Bartholomew. L. W. P. phot.

996. ARGENTON-CHÂTEAU, (Deux-Sèvres). Western portal, detail of voussures.
St. Bartholomew; an Apostle; foolish Virgins. L. W. P. phot.

997.   FENIOUX, (Charente-Inférieure).   Western façade.   Christ, six Apostles;
Zodiac; wise and foolish Virgins; Angels; Psychomachia. L. W. P. phot.

998. FENIOUX, (Charente-Inférieure). Western portal, detail of northern voussures. An Angel; Psychomachia. L. W. P. phot.

999. VARAIZE, (Charente-Inférieure). Voussures of the southern portal. Angels, Psychomachia. A. K. P. phot.

1000. VARAIZE, (Charente-Inférieure). Voussures of southern portal. Angels, Psychomachia. A. K. P. phot.

1001. VARAIZE, (Charente-Inférieure). Voussures of southern portal. An Angel,
Elders (?). L. W. P. phot.

1002. VARAIZE, (Charente-Inférieure). Voussures of southern portal. An Angel; Elders (?). L. W. P. phot.

1003. PONT-L'ABBÉ-D'ARNOULT, (Charente-Inférieure). Western façade, north-ern lunette. L. W. P. phot.

1004. Pont-l'Abbé-d'Arnoult, (Charente-Inférieure). Western façade, central tympanum. Wise and foolish Virgins; St. Catherine and other Saints; Psychomachia; Angels. L.W.P. phot.

1005. Pont-l'Abbé-d'Arnoult, (Charente-Inférieure). Western façade, south-ern lunette. Crucifixion of St. Peter. L. W. P. phot.

1006. St.-Michel, (Charente). Tympanum of portal. St. Michael and the Dragon.
I. W. P. phot.

1007. St.-Symphorien, (Charente-Inférieure). Western façade, upper register. Psychomachia. L. W. P. phot.

1008. Châteauneuf-sur-Charente, (Charente). Western façade, upper zone, northern lunette. Constantine and St. Helena. L. W. P. phot.

1009. CHÂTEAUNEUF-SUR-CHARENTE, (Charente). Western façade, relief north of central window. St. Peter. L. W. P. phot.

1010. CHÂTEAUNEUF-SUR-CHARENTE, (Charente). Western façade, upper zone, reliefs south of central window. A Sibyl (?) and a Prophet. L. W. P.

1011. MELLE, (Deux-Sèvres), St.-Hilaire. Northern portal. Constantine, fragments of Psychomachia and Zodiac. B.-A. phot.

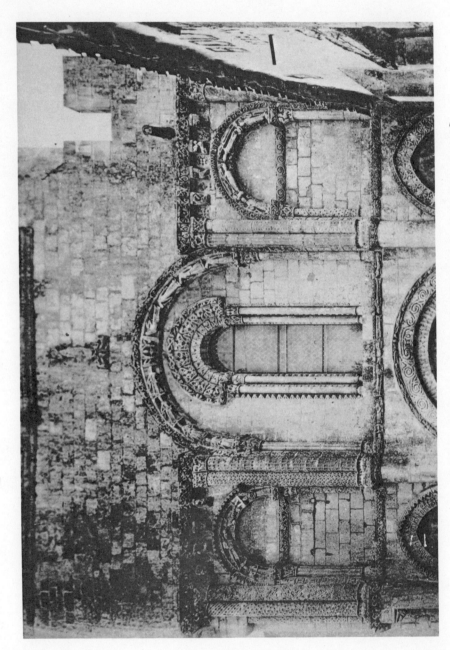

1012. CORME-ROYAL, (Charente-Inférieure). Western façade, upper zone. St. Michael, Saints; wise and foolish Virgins; Psychomachia. L. W. P.

1013. CORME-ROYAL, (Charente-Inférieure). Western façade, upper zone, northern lunette. St. Catherine, other Saints. L. W. P. phot.

1014. CORME-ROYAL, (Charente-Inférieure). Detail of voussure, central arch, upper story. The Foolish Virgins. L. W. P. phot.

1015. Corme-Royal, (Charente-Inférieure). Western façade, upper zone, southern lunette. Psychomachia. L. W. P. phot.

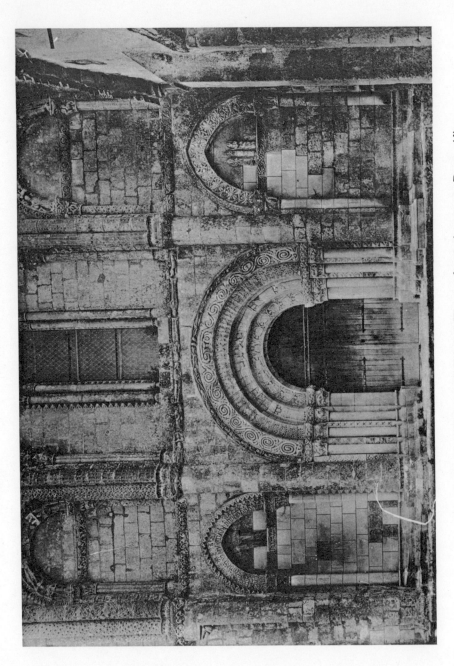

1016. CORME-ROYAL, (Charente-Inférieure). Western façade, lower part. Donors (?);

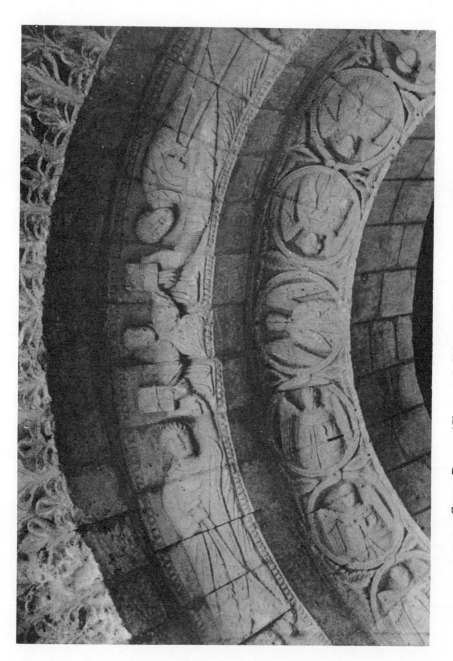

1017. CORME-ROYAL, (Charente-Inférieure). Voussures of central portal. Ecclesiastics, Angels. L. W. P. phot.

1018. Pérignac, (Charente-Inférieure). Western façade, upper zone. *Majestas Domini*. L. W. P. phot.

1019. PÉRIGNAC, (Charente-Inférieure). Western façade, upper gallery, northern
portion. Psychomachia. L. W. P. phot.

1020. PÉRIGNAC, (Charente-Inférieure). Western façade, upper gallery south of window. Psychomachia. L. W. P. phot.

1021. PÉRIGNAC, (Charente-Inférieure). Western façade, southern half, upper gallery. Psychomachia. L. W. P phot.

1022. PÉRIGNAC, (Charente-Inférieure). Western façade, lower gallery, northern portion. St Peter, three Apostles. I. W. P. phot.

1023. Pérignac, (Charente-Inférieure). Western façade, lower gallery, central portion. Christ, two Apostles. L. W. P. phot.

1024. Pérignac, (Charente-Inférieure). Western façade, lower gallery, southern

1025. RUFFEC, (Charente). Western façade, upper zone. The Ascension. L. W. P. phot.

1026. RUFFEC, (Charente). Western façade, middle zone, northern portion. Detail of the Ascension; four Apostles. J. W. P. phot.

1027. RUFFEC, (Charente). Western façade, middle zone, north of window. Detail of the Ascension; St. Peter. L. W. P. phot.

1028. RUFFEC, (Charente). Western façade, middle zone, south of window. Detail of the Ascension; two Apostles. L. W. P. phot.

1029. RUFFEC, (Charente). Western façade, northern lunette. Samson and Delilah. L. W. P. phot.

1030. Montmorillon, (Vienne). Octagone. Sculptures of façade. Luxury; other subjects. I. W. P. phot.

1031. MATHA, (Charente-Inférieure). Western façade, northern half, upper part.
Constantine. L. W. P. phot.

1032. MATHA, (Charente-Inférieure). Statue of façade, with head from elsewhere. L. W. P. phot.

1033. MATHA, (Charente-Inférieure). Statue of façade, with head from elsewhere. L. W. P. phot.

1034. Chadennac, (Charente-Inférieure). Western portal. 1140. L. W. P. phot.

1035. CHADENNAC, (Charente-Inférieure). Western portal, voussures. 1140.
I. W. P. phot.

1036. CHADENNAC, (Charente-Inférieure). Western portal, voussures. 1140.
L. W. P. phot.

1037. CHADENNAC, (Charente-Inférieure). Western façade, northern lunette.
Noble Donors (?), St. Hilaire (?). 1140. B.-A. phot.

1038. CHADENNAC, (Charente-Inférieure). Western façade, northern spandrel. A
Donor (?). 1140. L. W. P. phot.

1039. CHADENNAC, (Charente-Inférieure). Western façade, southern spandrel.
St. Michael. 1140. L. W. P. phot.

1040. Chadennac, (Charente-Inférieure). Western façade, southern end. St. Michael, St. Martin (?). 1140. L. W. P. phot.

1041. Blazimont, (Gironde). Western portal, voussure. Psychomachia. L. W. P.
phot.

1042.   BLAZIMONT, (Gironde). Western portal, voussure. Psychomachia. L. W. P.
        phot.

1043. BLAZIMONT, (Gironde). Western portal, voussure. An Angel. L. W. P. phot.

1044. BLAZIMONT, (Gironde). Western portal, detail of voussures. Psychomachia.
L. W. P. phot.

1045. PARTHENAY, (Deux-Sèvres), Notre-Dame-de-la-Couldre. Capital now in gate of adjoining school. David and Goliath. L. W. P. phot.

1046. PARTHENAY, (Deux-Sèvres), Notre-Dame-de-la-Couldre. Capital now in gate of adjoining school. The Sacrifice of Abraham. L. W. P. phot.

1047. PARTHENAY, (Deux-Sèvres), Notre-Dame-de-la-Couldre. Central portal, northern capital. L. W. P. phot.

1048. PARTHENAY, (Deux-Sèvres), Notre-Dame-de-la-Couldre. Western portal, Ella Porphyrnt; the Annunciation; the

1049. PARTHENAY, (Deux-Sèvres), Notre-Dame-de-la-Couldre. Western portal, voussures. Angels. L. W. P. phot.

1050. PARTHENAY, (Deux-Sèvres), Notre-Dame-de-la-Couldre. Western portal,
voussures. Psychomachia, Angels. L. W. P. phot.

1051. PARTHENAY, (Deux-Sèvres), Notre-Dame-de-la-Couldre. Western portal,
southern voussures. Elder, Psychomachia, Annunciation to Zacharias.
L. W. P. phot.

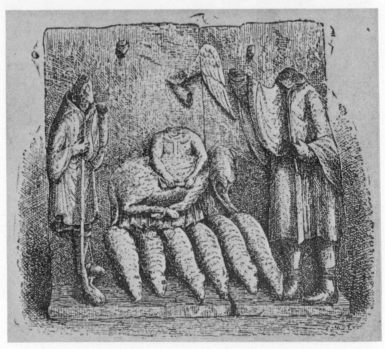

1052. PARTHENAY, (Deux-Sèvres), Notre-Dame-de-la-Couldre. Western façade, northern lunette. Constantine. A. K. P. phot.

1053. PARTHENAY, (Deux-Sèvres), Notre-Dame-de-la-Couldre. Fragment of frieze of western façade, now in Louvre. The Shepherds. From Sadoux' engraving, made before the restoration.

1054. PARTHENAY, (Deux-Sèvres), Notre-Dame-de-la-Couldre. Fragment of
frieze of western façade, now in Louvre. The Shepherds. Restored.
F. M. S. phot.

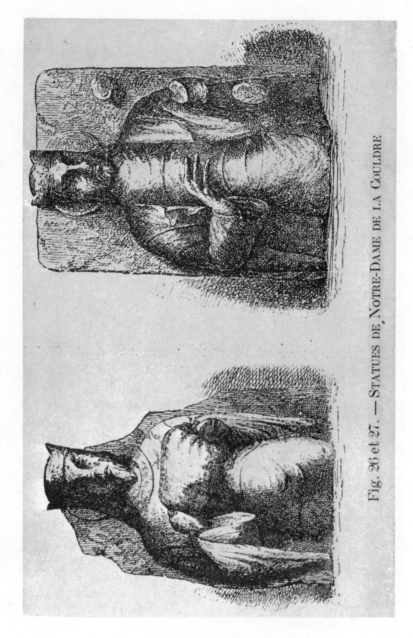

Fig. 26 et 27. — Statues de Notre-Dame de la Couldre

1055.   Parthenay, (Deux-Sèvres), Notre-Dame-de-la-Couldre.   Reliefs from western façade, now in Louvre.   An Elder.   From Sadoux' engraving.

1057. Parthenay, (Deux-Sèvres), Notre-Dame-de-la-Couldre. Reliefs from western façade, now in Louvre. Two Elders. Giraudon phot.

1058.   St.-Pompain, (Deux-Sèvres). Voussures of western portal. Psychomachia.
Signed by Giglelm. L. W. P. phot.

1059. THOUARS, (Deux-Sèvres), St.-Médard. Western façade. *Majestas Domini*; Apostles; Angels, Prophets, Saints, Entry into Jerusalem. Restored. L. W. P. phot.

1060. THOUARS, (Deux-Sèvres), St.-Médard. Western façade, detail. *Majestas*

1061. FOUSSAIS, (Vendée). Western façade, northern lunette. Deposition. Signed by Giraud Audebert of St.-Jean-d'Angély. L. W. P. phot.

1062. Foussais, (Vendée). Western façade, central portal. L. W. P. phot.

1063. FOUSSAIS, (Vendée). Western façade, southern lunette. *Noli me tangere.*
Feast at the House of Simon. L. W. P. phot.

1064. TROIS-PALIS, (Charente). Gable of western façade. *Majestas Domini.*
J. W. P. phot.

1065. MOREAUX, (Vienne). Portion of western façade with relief of a Bishop. c. 1140. A. K. P. phot.
1066. MOREAUX, (Vienne). Western portal, southern jamb. c. 1140. A. K. P. phot.

1067. Moreaux, (Vienne). Relief north of western portal. A Bishop. *c.* 1140.
L. W. P. phot.

1068. MOREAUX, (Vienne). Western façade, relief south of portal. A Bishop.
L. W. P. phot.

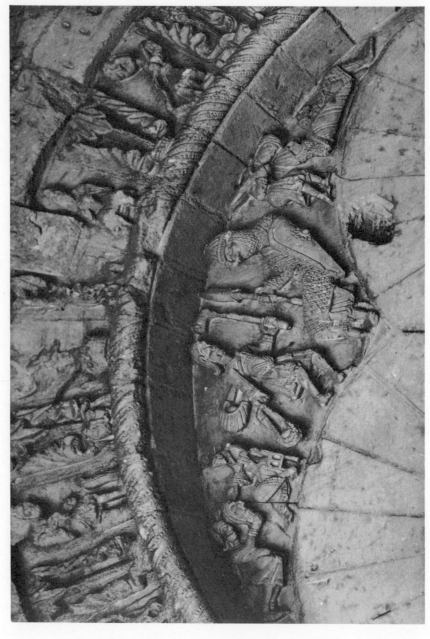

Ager. (Maine-et-Loire) St. Aubin. Voussures of cloister now in Préfec...

1070. ANGERS, (Maine-et-Loire), St.-Aubin. Arch of cloister, now in Préfecture. Angels, Virgin. Giraudon phot.

1071. ST.-SATURNIN, (Charente). Lunette of façade. Two Saints. L. W. P. phot.

1072. ST.-SATURNIN, (Charente). Lunette of façade. Christ and two Apostles. L. W. P. phot.

1072 a. MONTMORILLON, (Vienne), Eglise du Seminaire. Western façade, frieze. Annunciation, Nativity, Shepherds. L. W. P. phot.

1073. Montmorillon, (Vienne), Eglise du Seminaire. Western façade, frieze. Shepherds, Presentation, Adoration, Flight. L. W. P. phot.

1074. Selles-sur-Cher, (Loire-et-Cher). Sculptures in exterior of apse. L. W. P. phot.

1075. SELLES-SUR-CHER, (Loire-et-Cher). Relief of apse. St. Michael. L. W. P. phot.

1076. Selles-sur-Cher, (Loire-et-Cher). Relief in north wall of choir. The Visitation. A. K. P. phot.

1077. Selles-sur-Cher, (Loire-et-Cher). Apse, detail of lower frieze. The Nativity. A. K. P. phot.

1078. SELLES-SUR-CHER, (Loire-et-Cher). Apse, detail of lower frieze. The Resurrection of Lazarus. L. W. P. phot.

1079. SELLES-SUR-CHER, (LOIRE-ET-CHER). Apse, detail of lower frieze. The Last
Supper; Washing the Feet. B.-A. phot.

1080. SELLES-SUR-CHER, (Loire-et-Cher). Apse, detail of lower frieze. The Be-

trayal. J. W. P. phot.

1081. SELLES-SUR-CHER, (Loire-et-Cher). Apse, detail of lower frieze. Christ before Pilate. L. W. P. phot.

1082. SELLES-SUR-CHER, (Loire-et-Cher). Exterior of apse, detail of upper frieze.
St. Eusice's Sheep guarded by Wolves; the Miracle of the Bread. B.-A.

1083. VILLOGEN, (Charente). Relief south of western portal. Fall of the rebellious
Angels. L. W. P. phot.

VILLOGEN (Charente). Relief north of western portal. L. W. P. phot.

1085. St.-Vivien, (Gironde). Lunette of apse. L. W. P. phot.
1086. St.-Vivien, (Gironde). Lunette of apse. L. W. P. phot.

1087. CHALAIS, (Charente). Western façade. Prophets (?), three Saints (?); the
M............T.....L.W.P.phot

1088. CHALAIS, (Charente). Western façade, northern lunette. Three Saints (?). L. W. P. phot.

1089. Chalais, (Charente). Western façade, southern lunette. The Maries at the

1090. MELLE, (Deux-Sèvres). St.-Pierre. Relief over southern portal. Christ, St. Peter and St. Paul. L. W. P. phot.

1091. MELLE, (Deux-Sèvres). St.-Pierre. Capital of nave. Entombment of St. Hilaire. L. W. P. phot.

1092. SURGÈRES, (Charente-Inférieure). Western façade, northern upper lunette.
A Horseman. L. W. P. phot.

1093a. CAEN, (Calvados), St.-Etienne-le-Vieux. Relief in exterior of choir. Constantine (?).

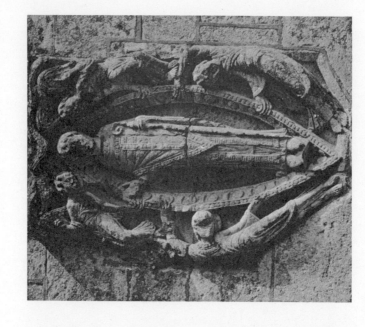

1094. GENSAC-LA-PALLUE, (Charente). Relief of western façade. The Virgin.
        L. W. P. phot.
1095. GENSAC-LA-PALLUE, (Charente). Relief of western façade. St. Ausone.
        L. W. P. phot.

1096. COGNAC, (Charente). Detail of voussures, western portal. July, August, September. L. W. P. phot.

1097. Aubeterre, (Charente), St.-Jacques. Western façade, detail of upper
arcading. Construction J. W. P. phot.

1098. AUBETERRE, (Charente), St.-Jacques. Western façade, northern lunette, frieze. May, April, March, February. L. W. P. phot.

1099. AUBETERRE, (Charente), St.-Jacques. Western façade, northern lunette, frieze. February, January, December. L. W. P. phot.

1100. L'ILE-BOUCHARD, (Indre-et-Loire), St.-Léonard. Capital of ambulatory.
The Baptism; Slaughter of the Innocents. L. W. P. phot.

1101. L'ILE-BOUCHARD, (Indre-et-Loire), St.-Léonard. Capital of ambulatory.
The Annunciation; the Visitation. L. W. P. phot.

1102. L'ILE-BOUCHARD, (Indre-et-Loire), St-Léonard. Capital of ambulatory.

1103. L'Ile-Bouchard, (Indre-et-Loire), St.-Léonard. Capital of ambulatory. The Entry into Jerusalem; the Temptation. L. W. P. phot.

1104. L'Ile-Bouchard, (Indre-et-Loire), St.-Léonard. Capital of ambulatory. The Last Supper. L. W. P. phot.

1105. L'Île-Bouchard, (Indre-et-Loire), St.-Léonard. Capital of ambulatory.

1106. L'ILE-BOUCHARD, (Indre-et-Loire), St.-Léonard. Capital of ambulatory.
      The Temptation. L. W. P. phot.
1107. L'ILE-BOUCHARD, (Indre-et-Loire), St.-Léonard. Capital of ambulatory.
      The Crucifixion, the Last Supper. L. W. P. phot.

1108. LOCHES, (Indre-et-Loire), St.-Ours. Console in choir. L. W. P. phot.

1109. LOCHES, (Indre-et-Loire), St.-Ours. Console in choir. A. K. P. phot.
1110. LOCHES, (Indre-et-Loire), St.-Ours. Console in choir. A. K. P. phot.

IIIII.   Loches, (Indre-et-Loire), St.-Ours.   Western portal.   Adoration of the Magi;

1112. Loches, (Indre-et-Loire), St.-Ours. Western portal, upper zone, northern portion. Adoration of the Magi. L. W. P. phot.

1113. LOCHES, (Indre-et-Loire), St.-Ours. Relief over western portal. Detail of the Adoration of the Magi. The Virgin and St. Joseph. L. W. P. phot.

1114. LOCHES, (Indre-et-Loire), St.-Ours. Western portal, upper zone, southern
portion. St. Joseph, the Magi. L. W. P. phot.

1115. LOCHES, (Indre-et-Loire), St.-Ours. Sculptured colonnettes embedded in western portal, middle zone, northern side. L. W. P. phot.

1116. Loches, (Indre-et-Loire), St.-Ours. Western portal, detail of voussures. Philosophy, Grammar. L. W. P. phot.

1117. LOCHES, (Indre-et-Loire), St.-Ours. Sculptured colonnettes embedded in western portal, middle zone, southern side. L. W. P. phot.

1118. LOCHES, (Indre-et-Loire), St.-Ours. Western portal, northern jamb. St. Ours. L. W. P. phot.

1119. LOCHES, (Indre-et-Loire), St.-Ours. Western portal, southern jamb. St. Peter. L. W. P. phot.

1120. LA VILLEDIEU, (Vienne). Relief of western façade. A Prophet. L. W. P. phot.

1121. LA VILLEDIEU, (Vienne). Relief of western façade. The Annunciation. L. W. P. phot.

1122. Civray, (Vienne), St.-Nicolas. Western façade, second story, northern spandrel. Two Prophets, Angels, Psychomachia. L. W. P. phot.

1123. CIVRAY, (Vienne), St.-Nicolas. Western façade, second story, northern spandrel. Two Prophets, Angels, Psychomachia. L. W. P. phot

1124. CIVRAY, (Vienne), St.-Nicolas. Western façade, second story, central window. Psychomachia, St. Paul, St. Peter. L. W. P. phot.

1125. CIVRAY, (Vienne), St.-Nicolas. Western façade, second story, southern spandrel. Two Prophets, Psychomachia, Prophets. L. W. P. phot.

1126. Civray, (Vienne), St.-Nicolas. Western façade, second zone, northern

1127. CIVRAY, (Vienne), St.-Nicolas. Western façade, second story, southern lunette. Prophets. L. W. P. phot.

1128. Civray, (Vienne), St.-Nicolas. Western façade, upper zone, southern lunette, lower portion. The Church, St. Nicolas and the three dowerless

1129. CIVRAY, (Vienne), St.-Nicolas. Western façade, upper zone, southern lunette, lower portion. Three dowerless Maidens and their Father (?), the Synagogue. L. W. P. phot.

1130. Civray, (Vienne), St.-Nicolas. Western portal, voussures. Virgin, Angels, Christ, wise Virgins. L. W. P. phot.

1131. Civray, (Vienne), St.-Nicolas. Western façade, central portal, voussures. Angel, foolish Virgins. L. W. P. phot.

1132. POITIERS, (Vienne), Musée des Antiquaires de l'Ouest. Fragment said to come from St.-Benoît. Four Apostles. L. W. P. phot.

1133. POITIERS, (Vienne), Musée des Antiquaires de l'Ouest. Fragment said to come from St.-Benoit. Three Apostles. L. W. P. phot.

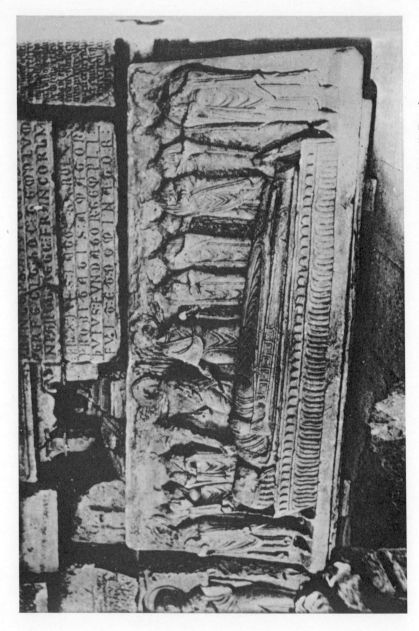

1134. POITIERS, (Vienne), St.-Hilaire-la-Celle. "Tombeau de St. Hilaire." Death of the Saint. F. M. S. phot. from cast.

1135. St.-Amand-de-Boixe, (Charente-Inférieure). Western portal, detail. F. M. S. phot.

1136.   Vouvant, (Vendée).   Façade of north transept.   The Last Supper; Samson and Delilah, Samson and the Lion.   L. W. P. phot.

1137. CROUZILLES, (Indre-et-Loire). Statue of façade. Restored. L. W. P. phot.
1138. CROUZILLES, (Indre-et-Loire). Statue of façade. L. W. P. phot.

ROMANESQUE SCULPTURE

OF THE PILGRIMAGE ROADS

VOLUME VIII

AUVERGNE AND DAUPHINE

ILLUSTRATIONS

ILLUSTRATIONS

(1139–1277)

AUVERGNE AND DAUPHINE

1158. CLERMONT-FERRAND, (Puy-de-Dôme), Notre-Dame-du-Port. Central portion of tympanum. *Majestas Domini*. L. W. P. phot.

1159. CLERMONT-FERRAND, (Puy-de-Dôme), Notre-Dame-du-Port. Tympanum of southern portal, western part. A Cherub. L. W. P. phot.

1160. CLERMONT-FERRAND, (Puy-de-Dôme), Notre-Dame-du-Port. Lintel of southern portal, eastern half. Adoration of the Magi. L. W. P. phot.

1161. CLERMONT-FERRAND, (Puy-de-Dôme), Notre-Dame-du-Port. Lintel of southern portal, eastern half. Presentation, Baptism. L. W. P. phot.

1162. CLERMONT-FERRAND, (Puy-de-Dôme), Notre-Dame-du-Port. Relief east of southern portal. Isaiah. L. W. P. phot.

1163. CLERMONT-FERRAND, (Puy-de-Dôme), Notre-Dame-du-Port. Relief east of southern portal. St. John the Baptist. L. W. P. phot.

1164. CLERMONT-FERRAND, (Puy-de-Dôme), Notre-Dame-du-Port. Relief west of southern portal. The Annunciation. L. W. P. phot.

1165. CLERMONT-FERRAND, (Puy-de-Dôme), Notre-Dame-du-Port. Capital of exterior of south transept. The Sacrifice of Isaac. L. W. P. phot.

1166. CLERMONT-FERRAND, (Puy-de-Dôme), Notre-Dame-du-Port. Relief east of south portal. The Nativity. L. W. P. phot.

1167. CLERMONT-FERRAND, (Puy-de-Dôme), Notre-Dame-du-Port. Capital of ambulatory. Resurrection of the Virgin. F. M. S. phot. from cast.

1168. CLERMONT-FERRAND, (Puy-de-Dôme), Notre-Dame-du-Port. Capital of ambulatory. Angel. F. M. S. phot. from cast.

1169. CLERMONT-FERRAND, (Puy-de-Dôme), Notre-Dame-du-Port. Capital of ambulatory. The Ark of the Covenant, symbol of the Virgin. F. M. S. phot. from cast.

1170. CLERMONT-FERRAND, (Puy-de-Dôme), Notre-Dame-du-Port. Capital of ambulatory. The Virgin as the Book of Life. F. M. S. phot. from cast.

1171. CLERMONT-FERRAND, (Puy-de-Dôme), Notre-Dame-du-Port. Capital of ambulatory. The Temptation. Giraudon phot. from cast.

1172. CLERMONT-FERRAND, (Puy-de-Dôme), Notre-Dame-du-Port. Capital of ambulatory. God reproaches Adam. F. M. S. phot. from cast.

1173. CLERMONT-FERRAND, (Puy-de-Dôme), Notre-Dame-du-Port. Capital of ambulatory. The Expulsion. F. M. S. phot. from cast.

1174. CLERMONT-FERRAND, (Puy-de-Dôme), Notre-Dame-du-Port. Capital of ambulatory. An Angel guards the Gates of Paradise. F. M. S. phot. from cast.

1175. CLERMONT-FERRAND, (Puy-de-Dôme), Notre-Dame-du-Port. Capital of ambulatory. The Annunciation. F. M. S. phot. from cast.

1176. CLERMONT-FERRAND, (Puy-de-Dôme), Notre-Dame-du-Port. Capital of ambulatory. Zacharias; Visitation. F. M. S. phot. from cast.

1177. CLERMONT-FERRAND, (Puy-de-Dôme), Notre-Dame-du-Port. Capital of ambulatory. Annunciation to Zacharias; Visitation. F. M. S. phot. from cast.

1178. CLERMONT-FERRAND, (Puy-de-Dôme), Notre-Dame-du-Port. Capital of ambulatory. Annunciation to Zacharias. F. M. S. phot. from cast.

1179. CLERMONT-FERRAND, (Puy-de-Dôme), Notre-Dame-du-Port. Capital of ambulatory. The Angel appears to Joseph. Signed by Rotbertus. Giraudon phot.

1180. CLERMONT-FERRAND, (Puy-de-Dôme), Notre-Dame-du-Port. Capital of ambulatory. Psychomachia; Charity *vs.* Avarice, Wisdom *vs.* Folly. F. M. S. phot. from cast.

1181. CLERMONT-FERRAND, (Puy-de-Dôme), Notre-Dame-du-Port. Capital of ambulatory. Wrath. F. M. S. phot. from cast.

1182. CLERMONT-FERRAND, (Puy-de-Dôme), Notre-Dame-du-Port. Capital of ambulatory. Psychomachia; Generosity and Avarice. F. M. S. phot. from cast.

1183. CLERMONT-FERRAND, (Puy-de-Dôme), Notre-Dame-du-Port. Capital of ambulatory. Etienne presents a Capital. F. M. S. phot.

1184. CLERMONT-FERRAND, (Puy-de-Dôme), Notre-Dame-du-Port. Capital of southern side aisle. The Temptation. F. M. S. phot.

1185. VIZILLE, (Isère). Chapelle du Cimetière, tympanum. *Majestas Domini;* the Last Supper. B.-A. phot.

1186. CHAMPAGNE, (Ardèche). Western portal, tympanum. Crucifixion. L. W. P. phot.

1187. VALENCE, (Drôme), Cathédrale. Tympanum of south transept. *Majestas Domini;* Miracle of Loaves and Fishes. A. K. P. phot.

1188. VALENCE, (Drôme), Cathédrale. Lintel of north transept. Magi before Herod, Adoration, Nativity, Annunciation. A. K. P. phot.

1189. VALENCE, (Drôme), Cathédrale. Tympanum of south transept. *Majestas Domini;* Miracle of Loaves and Fishes. B.-A.phot. from cast.

1190. ST.-NECTAIRE, (Puy-de-Dôme). Capital of ambulatory. The Maries at the Tomb. F. M. S. phot.

1191. ST.-NECTAIRE, (Puy-de-Dôme). Capital of ambulatory. The Elect in the Last Judgment. F. M. S. phot.

1192. ST.-NECTAIRE, (Puy-de-Dôme). Capital of ambulatory. Separation of the Elect and the Damned. F. M. S. phot.

1193. ST.-NECTAIRE, (Puy-de-Dôme). Capital of ambulatory. Horseman of the Apocalypse. F. M. S. phot.

1194. ST.-NECTAIRE, (Puy-de-Dôme). Capital of ambulatory. St. Nectaire is ordained. F. M. S. phot. from cast.

1195. ST.-NECTAIRE, (Puy-de-Dôme). Capital of ambulatory. St. Nectaire and the Devil on the Tiber. F. M. S. phot. from cast.

1196. ST.-NECTAIRE, (Puy-de-Dôme). Capital of ambulatory. Resurrection of St. Nectaire. F. M. S. phot. from cast.

1197. ST.-NECTAIRE, (Puy-de-Dôme). Capital of ambulatory. Resurrection of Bradulus. F. M. S. phot. from cast.

1198. St.-Nectaire, (Puy-de-Dôme). Capital of ambulatory. Resurrection of Bradulus; Resurrection of St. Nectaire. F. M. S. phot. from cast.

1199. St.-Nectaire, (Puy-de-Dôme). Capital of ambulatory. Giraudon phot. from cast.

1200. St.-Nectaire, (Puy-de-Dôme). Capital of ambulatory. Miracle of the Loaves and Fishes. Giraudon phot. from cast.

1201. St.-Nectaire, (Puy-de-Dôme). Capital of ambulatory. Miracle of the Loaves and Fishes; the Transfiguration. F. M. S. phot. from cast.

1202. St.-Nectaire, (Puy-de-Dôme). Capital of ambulatory. The Transfiguration. F. M. S. phot. from cast.

1203. St.-Nectaire, (Puy-de-Dôme). Capital of ambulatory. The Transfiguration. F. M. S. phot. from cast.

1204. St.-Nectaire, (Puy-de-Dôme). Capital of ambulatory. Carrying the Cross. F. M. S. phot.

1205. Clermont-Ferrand, (Puy-de-Dôme). Relief now in house, rue des Gras. Washing the Feet. B.-A. phot.

1206. Volvic, (Puy-de-Dôme). Console in choir. A. K. P. phot.

1207. Volvic, (Puy-de-Dôme). Angels Guardians of the Gift made to St. Priest by Guillaume de Bèze and his Wife. L. W. P. phot.

1208. Issoire, (Puy-de-Dôme), St.-Austremoine. Exterior of absidal chapel. Aries, Taurus and Gemini. F. M. S. phot.

1209. Issoire, (Puy-de-Dôme), St.-Austremoine. Relief of exterior of apse. Abraham and the three Angels. L. W. P. phot.

1210. Issoire, (Puy-de-Dôme), St.-Austremoine. Relief of exterior of apse. The Sacrifice of Isaac. L. W. P. phot.

1211. Issoire, (Puy-de-Dôme), St.-Austremoine. Relief in exterior of apse. Miracle of the Loaves and Fishes. L. W. P. phot.

1212. Issoire, (Puy-de-Dôme), St.-Austremoine. Capital of ambulatory. Carrying the Cross. A. K. P. phot.

1213. Issoire, (Puy-de-Dôme), St.-Austremoine. Capitals of ambulatory. *Domine quo vadis*. A. K. P. phot.

1214. Issoire, (Puy-de-Dôme), St.-Austremoine. Capital of ambulatory. The Last Supper. F. M. S. phot.

1214 a. Nantua, (Ain). Lintel of western portal. The Last Supper. A. K. P. phot.

1215. Vienne, (Isère), Cathédrale. Fragment in north vestibule. St. John. Silvestre phot.

1216. Vienne, (Isère), Cathédrale. Fragment in north vestibule. St. Peter. Silvestre phot.

1217. Vienne, (Isère), Cathédrale. Fragment in north vestibule. St. Paul. Silvestre phot.

1218. Vienne, (Isère), St.-André-le-Bas. Capital of nave. Job. By Guillaume de Martin, 1152. B.-A. phot. from cast.

1219. VIENNE, (Isère), St.-André-le-Bas. Capital of nave. Samson and the Lion. By Guillaume de Martin, 1152. B.-A. phot. from cast.

1219 a. VIENNE, (Isère), St.-Pierre. Relief of tympanum now in museum. St. Peter. Silvestre phot.

1220. LE PUY, (Haute-Loire), St.-Michel-de-l'Aiguille. Portal. Adoration of the Lamb; God. A. K. P. phot. from cast.

1221. YDES, (Cantal). North side of western porch. The Annunciation. A. K. P. phot.

1222. YDES, (Cantal). South side of western porch. Daniel and Habakkuk. A. K. P. phot.

1223. MOZAC, (Puy-de-Dôme). Tympanum in western façade of south transept. The Virgin, Saints and Donor. B.-A. phot.

1224. MOZAC, (Puy-de-Dôme). Capital in church. B.-A. phot.

1225. MOZAC, (Puy-de-Dôme). Capital in church. The Maries at the Tomb. B.-A. phot.

1226. MOZAC, (Puy-de-Dôme). Capital in church. The Maries at the Tomb. B.-A. phot.

1227. MOZAC, (Puy-de-Dôme). Capital in church. The Maries at the Tomb. B.-A. phot.

1228. DIE, (Drôme). Narthex, exterior, capital. Samson and the Lion. A. K. P. phot.

1229. DIE, (Drôme). Narthex, exterior, capital. Sacrifice of Isaac. A. K. P. phot.

1230. DIE, (Drôme), Cathédrale. Tympanum of western portal. The Crucifixion, the Evangelists. L. W. P. phot.

1231. LE PUY, (Haute-Loire), Hôtel Dieu. Columns now in museum. Charity; Queen of Sheba; St. Peter and Apostle; an Apostle (?). L. W. P. phot.

1232. LE PUY, (Haute-Loire), Hôtel Dieu. Column now in museum. An Apostle (?). L. W. P. phot.

1233. LE PUY, (Haute-Loire), Musée. Capitals. The Nativity. L. W. P. phot.

1234. ST.-BENOÎT-DU-SAULT, (Indre). Statue now in Musée de Berry, Bourges. A Bishop. L. W. P. phot.

1235. ST.-BENOÎT-DU-SAULT, (Indre). Statue now in Musée de Berry, Bourges. The Queen of Sheba. L. W. P. phot.

1236. GANAGOBIE, (Basses-Alpes). Tympanum of western portal. *Majestas Domini;* Apostles. B.-A. phot.

1237. GANAGOBIE, (Basses-Alpes). Cloister. A. K. P. phot.

1238. GANAGOBIE, (Basses-Alpes). Cloister, A. K. P. phot.

1239. LAVAUDIEU, (Haute-Loire). Capital of cloister. A. K. P. phot

1240. LAVAUDIEU, (Haute-Loire). Colonnette of cloister. A. K. P. phot.

1241. LUBERSAC, (Corrèze). Capital of exterior of apse. Burial of St. Stephen. L. W. P. phot.

1242. LUBERSAC, (Corrèze). Capital of exterior of apse. The Shepherds. L. W. P. phot.

1243. Lyon, (Rhône), Manécanterie. Detail of façade. A. K. P. phot.

1244. Lyon, (Rhône), Manécanterie. Relief of façade. A. K. P. phot.

1245. Lyon, (Rhône), Manécanterie. Relief of façade. A. K. P. phot.

1246. Mauriac, (Cantal). Tympanum of western portal, detail. The Ascension. L. W. P. phot.

1247. Mauriac, (Cantal). Tympanum of western portal, detail. The Ascension. L. W. P. phot.

1248. Mauriac, (Cantal). Baptismal font. A Saint, Baptism of Christ, St. Michael. A. K. P. phot.

1249. Mauriac, (Cantal). Western portal, base of southern jamb. A. K. P. phot.

1250. Chambon, (Puy-de-Dôme). Lintel of western portal. The Stoning of St. Stephen. L. W. P. phot.

1251. Meillers, (Allier). Lintel of western portal. Christ, Angels, Apostles. L. W. P. phot.

1252. Meillers, (Allier). Wooden statue in north absidiole. The Virgin. A. K. P. phot.

1253. Meillers, (Allier). Southern capital of western portal L'âne qui joue. A. K. P. phot.

1254. Ebreuil, (Allier), St.-Léger. Fragment of sculpture now in museum of Moulins. Christ. L. W. P. phot.

1255. Ebreuil, (Allier), St.-Léger. Relief now in museum of Moulins. St. John. L. W. P. phot.

1256. Ebreuil, (Allier), St.-Léger. Relief now in museum of Moulins. St. Paul. L. W. P. phot.

1257. St.-Menoux, (Allier). Sculptured fragments in porch. Majestas Domini; a Bishop. L. W. P. phot.

1258. St.-Menoux, (Allier). Fragments in narthex. Two Apostles. L. W. P. phot.

1259. St.-Menoux, (Allier). Fragment of relief now in museum of Moulins. Two Apostles. L. W. P. phot.

1260. Vigeois, (Corrèze). Relief east of northern portal. L. W. P. phot.

1261. Vigeois, (Corrèze). Relief west of northern portal. L. W. P. phot.

1262. Bourges, (Cher), St.-Pierre-le-Puellier. Tympanum now in Musée de Berry. Announcement of Death; Death of Virgin; Funeral; Burial; Assumption. L. W. P. phot.

1263. Bourges, (Cher), St.-Ursin. Tympanum of portal. The Fox as Schoolmaster, the Fox and Stork; the Fox and Chickens; a Bear; Hunting Scene; Zodiac. Signed by Girauldus. L. W. P. phot.

1264. Brioude, (Haute-Loire), St.-Julien. Capital of nave. F. M. S. phot.

1265. St.-Pons, (Hérault). Capital of cloister, now in Fogg Museum, Cambridge, Mass. The Feast at Emmaus. F. M. phot.

1266. St.-Pons, (Hérault). Capital of cloister, now in Fogg Museum, Cambridge, Mass. Preparation of the Feast in the House of Simon. F. M. phot.

1267. ST.-PONS, (Hérault). Capital of cloister, now in Museum of Fine Arts, Boston, Mass. The Annunciation to Zacharias. M. F. A. phot.

1268. ST.-PONS, (Hérault). Capital of cloister, now in court of University, Montpellier. The Crusade. A. K. P. phot.

1269. ST.-PONS, (Hérault). Capital of cloister, now in court of University, Montpellier. Crucifixion of St. Andrew. A. K. P. phot.

1270. ST.-PONS, (Hérault). Capital of cloister, now in Fogg Museum, Cambridge, Mass. *Majestas Domini.* F. M. phot.

1271. ST.-PONS, (Hérault). Capital of cloister, now in Fogg Museum, Cambridge, Mass. The Sacrament of Bread in the Old Law. F. M. phot.

1272. ST.-PONS, (Hérault). Capital of cloister, now in Metropolitan Museum, New York. Stoning of St. Stephen. M. M. A. phot.

1273. ST.-PONS, (Hérault). Capital of cloister, now in Metropolitan Museum, New York. The Princess of Trebizond. M. M. A. phot.

1274. ST.-PONS, (Hérault). Capital of cloister, now in museum of Toulouse. The Crucifixion. Lasalle phot.

1275. ST.-PIERRE-LE-MOÛTIER, (Nièvre). Tympanum of northern portal. *Majestas Domini;* Angels. L. W. P. phot.

1276. ST.-CHAMANT, (Corrèze). Tympanum of western portal. The Ascension. L. W. P. phot.

1277. CHISSEY, (Jura). Western portal, tympanum. Christ (?) at column, St. John and St. Peter. L. W. P. phot.

1139. THURET, (Puy-de-Dôme). Lintel of southern portal. Christ, St. Michael, St. Gabriel. L. W. P. phot.

1140. MARS, (Allier). Tympanum of western portal. *Majestas Domini*, Apostles.

L. W. P. phot.

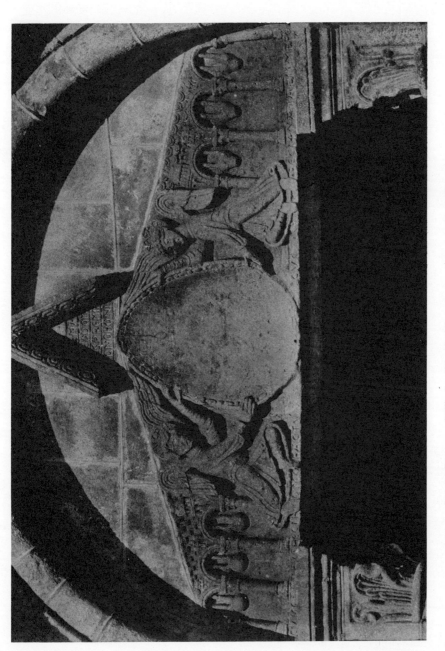

1141. Autry-Issard, (Allier). Lintel of western portal. St. Michael and St. Raphael. Signed by Natagis. L. W. P. phot.

1142. MARCILLAC, (Lot). Relief of southern portal. Christ. L. W. P. phot.

1143. MARCILLAC, (Lot). Relief of southern portal. St. Peter. L. W. P. phot.

1144. Marcillac, (Lot). Relief of southern portal. An Angel. L. W. P. phot.

1145. MARCILLAC, (Lot). Capital of cloister. *Majestas Domini*. A. K. P. phot.
1146. MARCILLAC, (Lot). Capital of narthex. Daniel. A. K. P. phot.

1147. St.-Pons, (Hérault). Tympanum of ancient portal. The Crucifixion.

1148. St.-Pons, (Hérault). Tympanum of ancient portal. The Last Supper.
L. W. P. phot.

1149. BOURG-ARGENTAL, (Loire). Western portal, detail. *Majestas Domini*;
...tion; Visitation; Nativity; Shepherds; Magi; David; Saints;

1150. BOURG-ARGENTAL, (Loire). Tympanum of western portal. *Majestas Domini;* Annunciation; Visitation; Nativity; Shepherds; Magi. L. W. P. phot.

1151. Bourg-Argental, (Loire). Western portal, northern jamb. Luxury, St.
James. L. W. P. phot.

1152. BOURG-ARGENTAL, (Loire). Western portal, southern jamb. Miraculous Draught of Fishes, Nebuchadnezzar, Charity, St. James the Less (?), Charity. L. W. P. phot.

1153. CHAMALIÈRES, (Haute-Loire). Holy-water basin. David, two Prophets.
L. W. P. phot.

1154. CHAMALIÈRES, (Haute-Loire). Holy-water basin. Two Prophets. L. W. P. phot.

1155. CHAMALIÈRES, (Haute-Loire). Detail of holy-water basin. A Prophet.
L. W. P. phot.

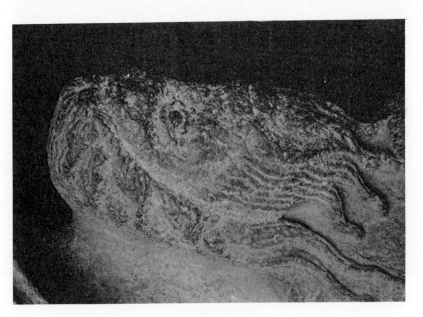

1156. CHAMALIÈRES, (Haute-Loire). Detail of holy-water basin. A Prophet. A. K. P. phot.

1157. CHAMALIÈRES, (Haute-Loire). Fragment of tomb in church. A. K. P. phot.

1158. CLERMONT-FERRAND, (Puy-de-Dôme), Notre-Dame-du-Port. Central portion of tympanum. *Majestas Domini.* L. W. P. phot.

1159.   CLERMONT-FERRAND, (Puy-de-Dôme), Notre-Dame-du-Port. Tympanum
of southern portal, western part. A Cherub. L. W. P. phot.

1160. Clermont-Ferrand, (Puy-de-Dôme), Notre-Dame-du-Port. Lintel of

1161. CLERMONT-FERRAND, (Puy-de-Dôme), Notre-Dame-du-Port. Lintel of southern portal, eastern half. Presentation, Baptism. L. W. P. phot.

1162. CLERMONT-FERRAND, (Puy-de-Dôme), Notre-Dame-du-Port. Relief east of southern portal. Isaiah. L. W. P. phot.

1163. CLERMONT-FERRAND, (Puy-de-Dôme), Notre-Dame-du-Port. Relief east of southern portal. St. John the Baptist. L. W. P. phot.

1164.   CLERMONT-FERRAND, (Puy-de-Dôme), Notre-Dame-du-Port.   Relief west of southern portal.   The Annunciation.   L. W. P. phot.

1165.   CLERMONT-FERRAND, (Puy-de-Dôme), Notre-Dame-du-Port.   Capital of exterior of south transept.   The Sacrifice of Isaac.   L. W. P. phot.

1167. CLERMONT-FERRAND, (Puy-de-Dôme), Notre-Dame-du-Port. Capital of ambulatory. Resurrection of the Virgin. F. M. S. phot. from cast.

1168. CLERMONT-FERRAND, (Puy-de-Dôme), Notre-Dame-du-Port. Capital of
ambulatory. Angel. F. M. S. phot. from cast.

1169. CLERMONT-FERRAND, (Puy-de-Dôme), Notre-Dame-du-Port. Capital of ambulatory. The Ark of the Covenant, symbol of the Virgin. F. M. S. phot. from cast.

1170. CLERMONT-FERRAND, (Puy-de-Dôme), Notre-Dame-du-Port. Capital of ambulatory. The Virgin as the Book of Life. F. M. S. phot. from cast.

1171. CLERMONT-FERRAND, (Puy-de-Dôme), Notre-Dame-du-Port. Capital of ambulatory. The Temptation. Giraudon phot. from cast.

1172. CLERMONT-FERRAND, (Puy-de-Dôme), Notre-Dame-du-Port. Capital of
ambulatory. God reproaches Adam. F. M. S. phot. from cast.

1173. CLERMONT-FERRAND, (Puy-de-Dôme), Notre-Dame-du-Port. Capital of ambulatory. The Expulsion. F. M. S. phot. from cast.

1174. CLERMONT-FERRAND, (Puy-de-Dôme), Notre-Dame-du-Port. Capital of ambulatory. An Angel guards the Gates of Paradise. F. M. S. phot. from cast.

1175. CLERMONT-FERRAND, (Puy-de-Dôme), Notre-Dame-du-Port. Capital of
ambulatory. The Annunciation. F. M. S. phot. from cast.

1176. CLERMONT-FERRAND, (Puy-de-Dôme), Notre-Dame-du-Port. Capital of ambulatory. Zacharias; Visitation. F. M. S. phot. from cast.

1177. CLERMONT-FERRAND, (Puy-de-Dôme), Notre-Dame-du-Port. Capital of
ambulatory. Annunciation to Zacharias; Visitation. F. M. S. phot.
from cast.

1178. CLERMONT-FERRAND, (Puy-de-Dôme), Notre-Dame-du-Port. Capital of
ambulatory. Annunciation to Zacharias. F. M. S. phot. from cast.

1179. CLERMONT-FERRAND, (Puy-de-Dôme), Notre-Dame-du-Port. Capital of ambulatory. The Angel appears to Joseph. Signed by Rotbertus. Giraudon phot.

1180. CLERMONT-FERRAND, (Puy-de-Dôme), Notre-Dame-du-Port. Capital of
ambulatory. Psychomachia; Charity *vs.* Avarice, Wisdom *vs.* Folly.
F. M. S. phot. from cast.

1181. CLERMONT-FERRAND, (Puy-de-Dôme), Notre-Dame-du-Port. Capital of
ambulatory. Wrath. F. M. S. phot. from cast.

1182. Clermont-Ferrand, (Puy-de-Dôme), Notre-Dame-du-Port. Capital of
ambulatory. Psychomachia; Generosity and Avarice. F. M. S. phot.
from cast.

1183. CLERMONT-FERRAND, (Puy-de-Dôme), Notre-Dame-du-Port. Capital of ambulatory. Etienne presents a Capital. F. M. S. phot.

1184. CLERMONT-FERRAND, (Puy-de-Dôme), Notre-Dame-du-Port. Capital of southern side aisle. The Temptation. F. M. S. phot.

1185. VIZILLE, (Isère). Chapelle du Cimetière, tympanum. *Majestas Domini;* the Last Supper. B.-A. phot.

1186. CHAMPAGNE, (Ardèche). Western portal, tympanum. Crucifixion.

1187. VALENCE, (Drôme), Cathédrale. Tympanum of south transept. *Majestas Domini;* Miracle of Loaves and Fishes. A. K. P. phot.

1188. VALENCE, (Drôme), Cathédrale. Lintel of north transept. Magi before Herod, Adoration, Nativity, Annunciation. A. K. P. phot.

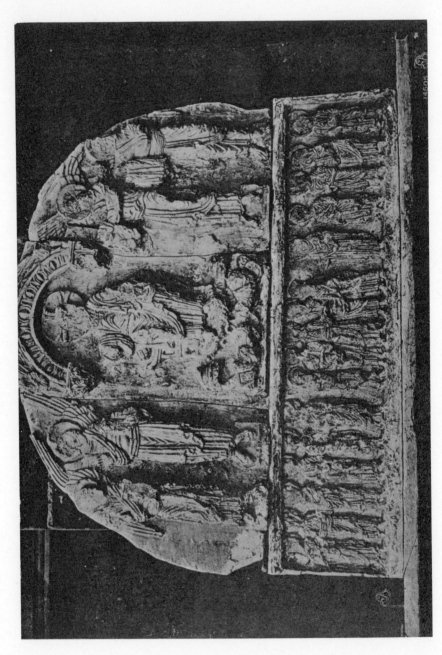

1189. VALENCE, (Drôme), Cathédrale. Tympanum of south transept. *Majestas Domini*: Miracle of Loaves and Fishes. B.-A. phot. from cast.

1190. ST.-NECTAIRE, (Puy-de-Dôme). Capital of ambulatory. The Maries at the
Tomb. F. M. S. phot.

1191. St.-Nectaire, (Puy-de-Dôme). Capital of ambulatory. The Elect in the
Last Judgment. F. M. S. phot.

1192. St.-Nectaire, (Puy-de-Dôme). Capital of ambulatory. Separation of the Elect and the Damned. F. M. S. phot.

1193. St.-Nectaire, (Puy-de-Dôme). Capital of ambulatory. Horseman of the Apocalypse. F. M. S. phot.

1194. St.-Nectaire, (Puy-de-Dôme). Capital of ambulatory. St. Nectaire is
ordained. F. M. S. phot. from cast.

1195. Sᴛ.-Nᴇᴄᴛᴀɪʀᴇ, (Puy-de-Dôme). Capital of ambulatory. St. Nectaire and the Devil on the Tiber. F. M. S. phot. from cast.

1196. St.-Nectaire, (Puy-de-Dôme). Capital of ambulatory. Resurrection of St. Nectaire. F. M. S. phot. from cast.

1197. St.-Nectaire, (Puy-de-Dôme). Capital of ambulatory. Resurrection of Bradulus. F. M. S. phot. from cast.

1198. St.-Nectaire, (Puy-de-Dôme). Capital of ambulatory. Resurrection of Bradulus; Resurrection of St. Nectaire. F. M. S. phot. from cast.

1199. ST.-NECTAIRE, (Puy-de-Dôme). Capital of ambulatory. Giraudon phot. from cast.

1200. ST.-NECTAIRE, (Puy-de-Dôme). Capital of ambulatory. Miracle of the Loaves and Fishes. Giraudon phot. from cast.

1201. St.-Nectaire, (Puy-de-Dôme). Capital of ambulatory. Miracle of the
Loaves and Fishes; the Transfiguration. F. M. S. phot. from cast.

1202. St.-Nectaire, (Puy-de-Dôme). Capital of ambulatory. The Transfiguration. F. M. S. phot. from cast.

1203. ST.-NECTAIRE, (Puy-de-Dôme). Capital of ambulatory. The Transfiguration. F. M. S. phot. from cast.

1204. St.-Nectaire, (Puy-de-Dôme). Capital of ambulatory. Carrying the Cross. F. M. S. phot.

1205. CLERMONT-FERRAND, (Puy-de-Dôme). Relief now in house, rue des Gras. Washing the Feet. B.-A. phot.

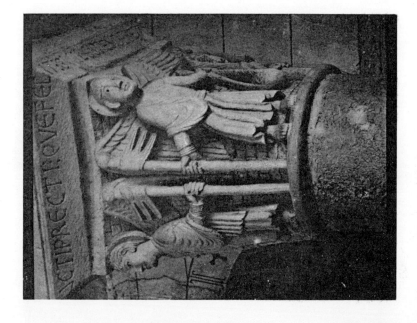

1206. VOLVIC, (Puy-de-Dôme). Console in choir. A. K. P. phot.
1207. VOLVIC, (Puy-de-Dôme). Angels Guardians of the Gift made to St. Priest
by Guillaume de Bèze and his Wife. L. W. P. phot.

1208. Issoire, (Puy-de-Dôme), St.-Austremoine. Exterior of absidal chapel.
Aries, Taurus and Gemini. F. M. S. phot.

1209. ISSOIRE, (Puy-de-Dôme), St.-Austremoine. Relief of exterior of apse. Abra-
       ham and the three Angels. L. W. P. phot.

1210. ISSOIRE, (Puy-de-Dôme), St.-Austremoine. Relief of exterior of apse. The
       Sacrifice of Isaac. L. W. P. phot.

1211. ISSOIRE, (Puy-de-Dôme), St.-Austremoine. Relief in exterior of apse. Miracle of the Loaves and Fishes. L. W. P. phot.

1212. ISSOIRE, (Puy-de-Dôme), St.-Austremoine. Capital of ambulatory. Carrying the Cross. A. K. P. phot.

1213. ISSOIRE, (Puy-de-Dôme), St.-Austremoine. Capitals of ambulatory. *Domine*

1214. ISSOIRE, (Puy-de-Dôme), St.-Austremoine. Capital of ambulatory. The Last Supper. F. M. S. phot.

1214 a. NANTUA, (Ain). Lintel of western portal. The Last Supper. A. K. P.

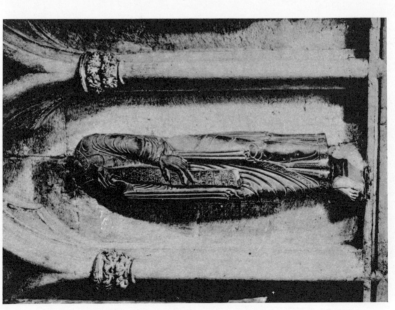

1215. VIENNE, (Isère), Cathédrale. Fragment in north vestibule. St. John. Silvestre phot.

1216. VIENNE, (Isère), Cathédrale. Fragment in north vestibule. St. Peter. Silvestre phot.

1217. VIENNE, (Isère), Cathédrale. Fragment in north vestibule. St. Paul. Silvestre phot.

1218. VIENNE, (Isère), St.-André-le-Bas. Capital of nave. Job. By Guillaume de
Martin, 1152. B.-A. phot. from cast.

1219. VIENNE, (Isère), St.-André-le-Bas. Capital of nave. Samson and the Lion.
By Guillaume de Martin, 1152. B.-A. phot. from cast.

1219 a. Vienne, (Isère), St.-Pierre. Relief of tympanum now in museum. St. Peter.
Silvestre phot.

1220. LE PUY, (Haute-Loire), St.-Michel-de-l'Aiguille. Portal. Adoration of the

1221. YDES, (Cantal). North side of western porch. The Annunciation. A. K. P. phot.

1222. YDES, (Cantal). South side of western porch. Daniel and Habakkuk.

1223.   MOZAC, (Puy-de-Dôme).   Tympanum in western façade of south transept.
The Virgin, Saints and Donor.   B.-A. phot.

1224. MOZAC, (Puy-de-Dôme). Capital in church. B.-A. phot.

1225. Mozac, (Puy-de-Dôme). Capital in church. The Maries at the Tomb.
B.-A. phot.

1226. Mozac, (Puy-de-Dôme). Capital in church. The Maries at the Tomb. B.-A. phot.

1227. MOZAC, (Puy-de-Dôme). Capital in church. The Maries at the Tomb.
B.-A. phot.

1228. DIE, (Drôme). Narthex, exterior, capital. Samson and the Lion. A. K. P. phot.

1230. Die, (Drôme), Cathédrale. Tympanum of western portal. The Crucifixion, the Evangelists. L. W. P. phot.

1231. LE PUY, (Haute-Loire), Hôtel Dieu. Columns now in museum. Charity; Queen of Sheba; St. Peter and Apostle; an Apostle (?). L. W. P. phot.

1232. LE PUY, (Haute-Loire), Hôtêl Dieu. Column now in museum. An
Apostle (?). L. W. P. phot.

1233. LE PUY, (Haute-Loire), Musée. Capitals. The Nativity. L. W. P. phot.

1234. St.-Benoît-du-Sault, (Indre). Statue now in Musée de Berry, Bourges.
A Bishop. L. W. P. phot.
1235. St.-Benoît-du-Sault, (Indre). Statue now in Musée de Berry, Bourges.
The Queen of Sheba. L. W. P. phot.

1236. GANAGOBIE, (Basses-Alpes). Tympanum of western portal. *Majestas Domini*; Apostles. B.-A. phot.

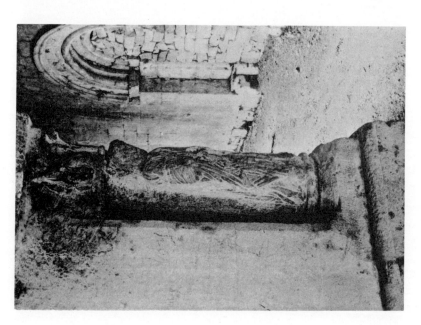

1237. GANAGOBIE, (Basses-Alpes). Cloister. A. K. P. phot.
1238. GANAGOBIE, (Basses-Alpes). Cloister, A. K. P. phot.

1239. LAVAUDIEU, (Haute-Loire). Capital of cloister. A. K. P. phot
1240. LAVAUDIEU, (Haute-Loire). Colonnette of cloister. A. K. P. phot.

1241. LUBERSAC, (Corrèze). Capital of exterior of apse. Burial of St. Stephen.
  L. W. P. phot.
1242. LUBERSAC, (Corrèze). Capital of exterior of apse. The Shepherds. L. W. P.
  phot.

1243.　Lyon, (Rhône), Manécanterie.　Detail of façade.　A. K. P. phot.

1244. Lyon, (Rhône), Manécanterie. Relief of façade. A. K. P. phot.
1245. Lyon, (Rhône), Manécanterie. Relief of façade. A. K. P. phot.

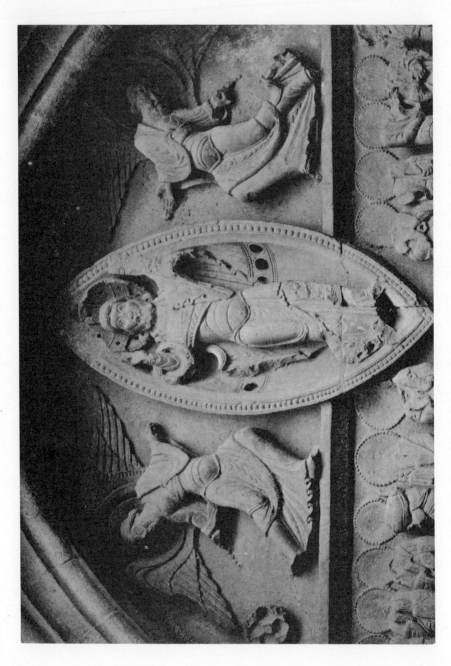

1246. MAURIAC, (Cantal). Tympanum of western portal, detail. The Ascension.
L. W. P. phot.

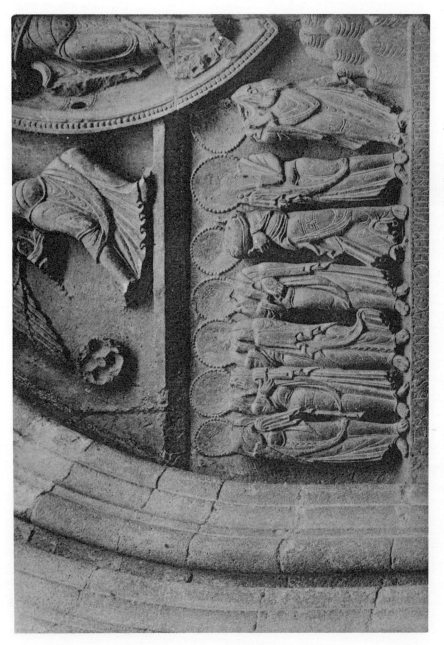

1247. MAURIAC, (Cantal). Tympanum of western portal, detail. The Ascension.
L. W. P. phot.

1248. MAURIAC, (Cantal). Baptismal font. A Saint, Baptism of Christ, St. Michael. A. K. P. phot.

1249. MAURIAC, (Cantal). Western portal, base of southern jamb. A. K. P. phot.

1250.   CHAMBON, (Puy-de-Dôme). Lintel of western portal. The Stoning of St. Stephen. L. W. P. phot.

1251. MEILLERS, (Allier). Lintel of western portal. Christ, Angels, Apostles.

L. W. D. phot.

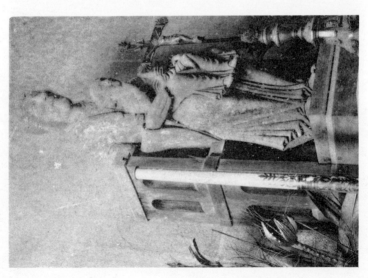

1252. MEILLERS, (Allier). Wooden statue in north absidiole. The Virgin. A. K. P. phot.

1253. MEILLERS, (Allier). Southern capital of western portal *L'âne qui joue.* A. K. P. phot.

1254. EBREUIL, (Allier), St.-Léger. Fragment of sculpture now in museum of Moulins. Christ. L. W. P. phot.

1255. EBREUIL, (Allier), St.-Léger. Relief now in museum of Moulins. St. John.
L. W. P. phot.
1256. EBREUIL, (Allier), St.-Léger. Relief now in museum of Moulins. St. Paul.
L. W. P. phot.

1257. St.-Menoux, (Allier). Sculptured fragments in porch. *Majestas Domini;* a Bishop. L. W. P. phot.

1258. St.-Menoux, (Allier). Fragments in narthex. Two Apostles. L. W. P. phot.

1259. St.-Menoux, (Allier). Fragment of relief now in museum of Moulins. Two Apostles. L. W. P. phot.

1260. Vigeois, (Corrèze). Relief east of northern portal. L. W. P. phot.
1261. Vigeois, (Corrèze). Relief west of northern portal. L. W. P. phot.

1262. BOURGES, (Cher), St.-Pierre-le-Puellier. Tympanum now in Musée de

1263. BOURGES, (Cher), St.-Ursin. Tympanum of portal. The Fox as Schoolmaster, the Fox and Stork; the Fox and Chickens; a Bear; Hunting
Scene; Zodiac. Signed by Girauldus. L. W. P. phot.

1264. Brioude, (Haute-Loire), St.-Julien. Capital of nave. F. M. S. phot.

1265. St.-Pons, (Hérault). Capital of cloister, now in Fogg Museum, Cambridge, Mass. The Feast at Emmaus. F. M. phot.

1266.   St.-Pons, (Hérault). Capital of cloister, now in Fogg Museum, Cambridge,
Mass. Preparation of the Feast in the House of Simon. F. M. phot.

1267. Sᴛ.-Pᴏɴs, (Hérault). Capital of cloister, now in Museum of Fine Arts, Boston, Mass. The Annunciation to Zacharias. M. F. A. phot.

1268. St.-Pons, (Hérault). Capital of cloister, now in court of University, Montpellier. The Crusade. A. K. P. phot.

1269.   ST.-PONS, (Hérault). Capital of cloister, now in court of University, Montpellier. Crucifixion of St. Andrew. A. K. P. phot.

1270. Sᴛ.-Pᴏɴs, (Hérault). Capital of cloister, now in Fogg Museum, Cambridge, Mass. *Majestas Domini*. F. M. phot.

1271. St.-Pons, (Hérault). Capital of cloister, now in Fogg Museum, Cambridge, Mass. The Sacrament of Bread in the Old Law. F. M. phot.

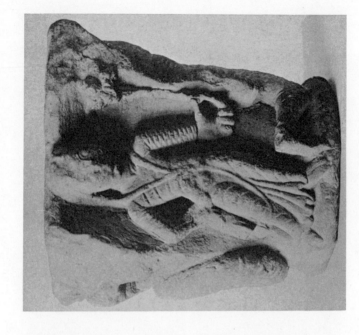

1272.   St.-Pons, (Hérault).   Capital of cloister, now in Metropolitan Museum,
            New York. Stoning of St. Stephen. M. M. A. phot.

1273.   St.-Pons, (Hérault).   Capital of cloister, now in Metropolitan Museum,
            New York. The Princess of Trebizond. M. M. A. phot.

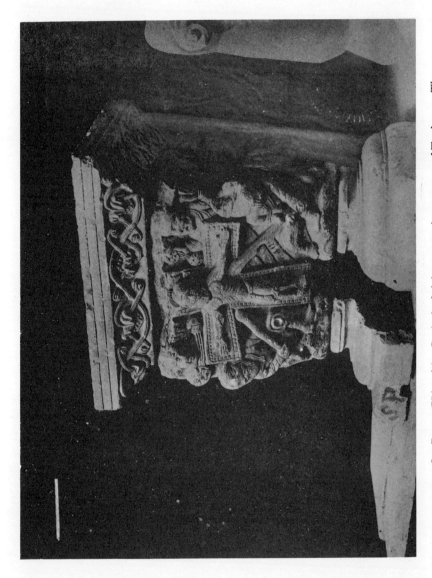

1274. St.-Pons, (Hérault). Capital of cloister, now in museum of Toulouse. The
Crucifixion. Lasalle phot.

1275. St.-Pierre-le-Moûtier, (Nièvre). Tympanum of northern portal. *Ma-iestas Domini*: Angels. L. W. P. phot.

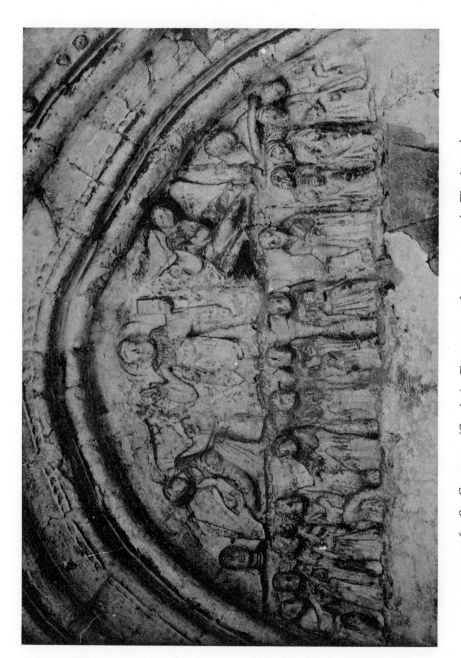

1276. St.-Chamant, (Corrèze). Tympanum of western portal. The Ascension.
L. W. P. phot.

1277. CHISSEY, (Jura). Western portal, tympanum. Christ (?) at column, St.
[...] W. P. phot.

ROMANESQUE SCULPTURE

OF THE PILGRIMAGE ROADS

VOLUME IX

PROVENCE

ILLUSTRATIONS

ILLUSTRATIONS

(1278–1410)

PROVENCE

1278. MARSEILLE, (Bouches-du-Rhône), St.-Victor. Tomb of St. Isarne, † 1048, now in museum. Giraudon phot. from cast.

1279. REGENSBURG, (Bavaria), St.-Emmeran. Relief now south of western portal. Christ. 1049-1064. Stoedtner phot.

1280. REGENSBURG, (Bavaria), St.-Emmeran. Relief now south of western portal. Christ. 1049-1064. Stoedtner phot.

1281. REGENSBURG, (Bavaria), St.-Emmeran. Relief now flanking western portals. St. Emmeran. Stoedtner phot.

1282. REGENSBURG, (Bavaria), St.-Emmeran. Relief now flanking western portals. St. Dionysus. Stoedtner phot.

1283. MARSEILLE, (Bouches-du-Rhône), Cathédrale Ancienne. Altar-frontal, detail. St. Cannate. 1122. A. K. P. phot.

1284. MARSEILLE, (Bouches-du-Rhône), Cathédrale Ancienne. Altar-frontal, detail. The Virgin. 1122. A. K. P. phot.

1285. MAGUELONNE, (Hérault), Cathédrale. Southern transept, western portal, northern corbel. St. Peter. A. K. P. phot.

1286. MAGUELONNE, (Hérault), Cathédrale. Southern transept, western portal, southern corbel. St. Paul. A. K. P. phot.

1287. MAGUELONNE, (Hérault), Cathédrale. Relief south of western portal, southern transept. St. Peter. A. K. P. phot. from cast.

1288. MAGUELONNE, (Hérault),' Cathédrale. Relief north of western portal, southern transept. St. Paul. L. W. P. phot.

1289. ST.-HILAIRE, (Aude). Tombeau de St. Hilaire. St. Hilaire is arrested. L. W. P. phot.

1290. ST.-HILAIRE, (Aude). Tombeau de St. Hilaire. Martyrdom of St. Saturnin. A. K. P. phot.

1291. ST.-GABRIEL, (Bouches-du-Rhône). Relief of western façade. The Annunciation; the Visitation. L. W. P. phot.

1292. BEAUCAIRE, (Gard), Notre-Dame-des-Pommiers. Frieze now in southern façade. Washing the Feet; Last Supper; Judas receives the Price of his Treason; Executioners. A. K. P. phot.

1293. BEAUCAIRE, (Gard), Notre-Dame-des-Pommiers. Frieze now in southern façade, detail. Peter denies Christ; Washing the Feet, Last Supper. A. K. P. phot. from cast.

1294. BEAUCAIRE, (Gard), Notre-Dame-des-Pommiers. Frieze now in southern façade, detail. Last Supper. A. K. P. phot. from cast.

1295. BEAUCAIRE, (Gard), Notre-Dame-des-Pommiers. Frieze now in southern façade, detail. Last Supper, Judas receives the Price of his Treason, Betrayal. A. K. P. phot. from cast.

1296. BEAUCAIRE, (Gard), Notre-Dame-des-Pommiers. Frieze now in southern façade, detail. Betrayal, Christ before Pilate, Flagellation. A. K. P. phot. from cast.

1297. BEAUCAIRE, (Gard), Notre-Dame-des-Pommiers. Frieze now in southern façade, detail. Flagellation, Executioners. A. K. P. phot. from cast.

1298. BEAUCAIRE, (Gard), Notre-Dame-des-Pommiers. Frieze now in southern façade, detail. Carrying the Cross; the Maries buying Spices; the Maries at the Tomb. A. K. P. phot. from cast.

1299. BEAUCAIRE, (Gard), Notre-Dame-des-Pommiers. Virgin of the Adoration, from tympanum, now in house of priest. L. W. P. phot.

1300. ST.-GUILHEM-LE-DÉSERT, (Hérault). Altar-frontal. *Majestas Domini*, Crucifixion. L. W. P. phot.

1301. FONTFROIDE, (Aude). Relief now in court of university. Montpellier. Adoration of the Magi. A. K. P. phot.

1302. ST.-GILLES, (Gard). Western façade, statue south of northern portal. St. Matthew. Signed by Brunus. A. K. P. phot.

1303. ST.-GILLES, (Gard). Western façade, second statue south of northern portal. St. Bartholomew. A. K. P. phot.

1304. ST.-GILLES, (Gard). Western façade, second statue north of central portal. St. Thomas. A. K. P. phot.

1305. ST.-GILLES, (Gard). Western façade, relief north of central portal. St. James the Less. A. K. P. phot.

1306. ST.-GILLES, (Gard). Northern jamb of central portal, western façade. Detail of St. John. A. K. P. phot.

1307. ST.-GILLES, (Gard). Northern jamb of central portal, western façade. Detail of St. John. A. K. P. phot.

1308. ST.-GILLES, (Gard). Northern jamb of central portal, western façade. Detail of St. Peter. A. K. P. phot.

1309. ST.-GILLES, (Gard). Northern jamb of central portal, western façade. Detail of St. Peter. A. K. P. phot.

1310. ST.-GILLES, (Gard). Western façade, southern jamb of central portal. Detail of St. James the Less. A. K. P. phot.

1311. ST.-GILLES, (Gard). Western façade, southern jamb of central portal. Detail of St. Paul. A. K. P. phot.

1312. ST.-GILLES, (Gard). Western façade, reliefs south of central portal. Two Apostles.

1313. ST.-GILLES, (Gard). Western façade, relief south of central portal, detail. An Apostle. Stoedtner phot.

1314. ST.-GILLES, (Gard). Western façade, statues north of southern portal. Two Apostles. A. K. P. phot.

1315. St.-Gilles, (Gard). Western façade, frieze north of central portal. The Money-Changers; they are driven from the Temple; Martha and Mary supplicate Christ; Raising of Lazarus; St. Bartholomew, St. Thomas, St. James the Less. Giraudon phot. from cast.

1316. St.-Gilles, (Gard). Western façade, frieze north of central portal. The Money-Changers; they are driven from the Temple; Martha and Mary supplicate Christ; Raising of Lazarus. F. M. S. phot. from cast.

1317. St.-Gilles, (Gard). Western façade, frieze north of central portal. The Money-Changers driven from the Temple; Martha and Mary supplicate Christ; Raising of Lazarus. Stoedtner phot.

1318. St.-Gilles, (Gard). Western façade, lintel of central portal. The Last Supper. A. K. P. phot.

1319. St.-Gilles, (Gard). Western façade, frieze in reveal south of central portal. Detail of the Betrayal. Stoedtner phot.

1320. St.-Gilles, (Gard). Western façade, frieze in reveal south of central portal. Detail of the Betrayal. A. K. P. phot. from cast.

1321. St.-Gilles, (Gard). Western façade, frieze south of central portal. Christ before Pilate; the Flagellation. F. M. S. phot.

1322. St.-Gilles, (Gard). Western façade, frieze south of central portal. Pilate; the Flagellation. Giraudon phot. from cast.

1323. St.-Gilles, (Gard), Abbaye. Detail of architrave south of central portal. Stoedtner phot.

1324. St.-Gilles, (Gard). Western façade, socle north of central portal. The Murder of Abel. Stoedtner phot.

1325. St.-Gilles, (Gard). Western façade, socle north of central portal. The Sacrifices of Cain and Abel. A. K. P. phot.

1325 a. St.-Gilles, (Gard). Western façade, podium north of central portal. F. M. S. phot. from cast.

1325 b. St.-Gilles, (Gard). Western façade, podium south of central portal. F. M. S. phot. from cast.

1326. St.-Gilles, (Gard). Western façade, socle south of central portal. David and Goliath. A. K. P. phot.

1327. St.-Gilles, (Gard). Western façade, socle south of central portal. The Angel of the Lord appears to David; Samson. A. K. P. phot.

1328. St.-Gilles, (Gard). Western façade, socle south of central portal. A. K. P. phot.

1329. St.-Gilles, (Gard). Fragment now in ruins of choir. Adoration of the Magi. A. K. P. phot.

1330. St.-Gilles, (Gard). Vaults of crypt, key-stone. The Deity. Stoedtner phot.

1331. Aix-en-Provence, (Bouches-du-Rhône), Cathédrale. Relief in choir. A. K. P. phot.

1332. Montmajour, (Bouches-du-Rhône). Relief west of portal in cloister. L. W. P. phot.

1333. Montmajour, (Bouches-du-Rhône). Relief east of portal in cloister. L. W. P. phot.

1334. Romans, (Drôme), St.-Barnard. Western portal, northern jamb. St. Peter, St. James. B.-A. phot.

1335. Romans, (Drôme), St.-Barnard. Western portal, southern jamb. St. John, St. Paul. L. W. P. phot.

1336. Romans, (Drôme), St.-Barnard. Capital of western portal. The Journey to Emmaus. L. W. P. phot.

1337. Romans, (Drôme), St.-Barnard. Western portal, capital. L. W. P. phot.

1338. Romans, (Drôme), St.-Barnard. Capital of nave. The Annunciation. L. W. P. phot.

1339. Avignon, (Vaucluse), Notre-Dame-des-Doms. Episcopal throne composed with ancient fragments. St. Mark. Silvestre phot.

1340. Avignon, (Vaucluse), Notre-Dame-des-Doms. Episcopal throne composed of ancient fragments. St. Luke. Silvestre phot.

1341. Avignon, (Vaucluse). Musée Calvet. Capital. Job. Silvestre phot.

1342. Avignon, (Vaucluse), Notre-Dame-des-Doms. Capital of cloister, now in Fogg Museum, Cambridge, Mass. Samson and the Lion. F. M. phot.

1343. Avignon, (Vaucluse), Notre-Dame-des-Doms. Capital of cloister, now in Fogg Museum, Cambridge, Mass. Delilah cuts Samson's Hair. F. M. phot.

1344. Arles, (Bouches-du-Rhône), St.-Trophîme. North-west pier of cloister. St. John. L. W. P. phot.

1345. Arles, (Bouches-du-Rhône), St.-Trophîme. North-west pier of cloister. St. Trophîme. F. M. S. phot. from cast.

1346. Arles, (Bouches-du-Rhône), St.-Trophîme. Detail of north-west pier of cloister. St. Trophîme. Stoedtner phot.

1347. Arles, (Bouches-du-Rhône), St.-Trophîme. North-west pier of cloister. St. Peter. A. K. P. phot.

1348. Arles, (Bouches-du-Rhône), St.-Trophîme. Detail of north-west pier of cloister. Detail of St. Peter. Stoedtner phot.

1349. Arles, (Bouches-du-Rhône), St.-Trophîme. Northern gallery of cloister, first pier. St. James, a Pilgrim. L. W. P. phot.

1350. Arles, (Bouches-du-Rhône), St.-Trophîme. Northern gallery of cloister, first pier. St. James, a Pilgrim. A. K. P. phot.

1351. Arles, (Bouches-du-Rhône), St.-Trophîme. Northern gallery of cloister, second pier. Doubting Thomas. A. K. P. phot.

1352. Arles, (Bouchès-du-Rhône), St.-Trophîme. Northern gallery of cloister, second pier. St. James the Less. A. K. P. phot.

1353. Arles, (Bouches-du-Rhône), St.-Trophîme. North-east pier of cloister. St. Paul, the Ascension, St. Stephen. L. W. P. phot.

1354. Arles, (Bouches-du-Rhône), St.-Trophîme. North-east pier of cloister. St. Stephen. A. K. P. phot.

1355. ARLES, (Bouches-du-Rhône), St.-Trophîme. North-east pier of cloister. St. Matthew; Passion of St. Stephen. A. K. P. phot.

1356. ARLES, (Bouches-du-Rhône), St.-Trophîme. North-east pier of cloister. St. Stephen, Passion of St. Stephen, St. Matthew. L. W. P. phot.

1357. ARLES, (Bouches-du-Rhône), St.-Trophîme. Eastern gallery of cloister, first pier. Judas (?). A. K. P. phot.

1358. ARLES, (Bouches-du-Rhône), St.-Trophîme. Eastern gallery of cloister, second pier. The Queen of Sheba. A. K. P. phot.

1359. ARLES, (Bouches-du-Rhône), St.-Trophîme. Eastern gallery of cloister, second pier. Solomon. L. W. P. phot.

1360. ARLES, (Bouches-du-Rhône), St.-Trophîme. Capital of east gallery of cloister. Entry into Jerusalem; Conversion of St. Paul. A. K. P. phot.

1361. ARLES, (Bouches-du-Rhône), St.-Trophîme. Reliefs of south-east pier of cloister. Washing the Feet, Last Supper, Betrayal. A. K. P. phot.

1362. ARLES, (Bouches-du-Rhône), St.-Trophîme. South-east pier of cloister. Gamaliel. A. K. P. phot.

1363. ARLES, (Bouches-du-Rhône), St.-Trophîme. Holy-water basin at south-east angle of cloister. L. W. P. phot.

1364. ARLES, (Bouches-du-Rhône), St.-Trophîme. Holy-water basin at south-east angle of cloister. A. K. P. phot.

1365. ARLES, (Bouches-du-Rhône), St.-Trophîme. Relief of south-east pier of cloister. The Temptation. A. K. P. phot.

1366. ARLES, (Bouches-du-Rhône), St.-Trophîme. Western façade. The Last Judgment. B.-A. phot.

1367. ARLES, (Bouches-du-Rhône), St.-Trophîme. Western façade, northern end. The Temptation; Psychostasy. L. W. P. phot.

1368. ARLES, (Bouches-du-Rhône), St.-Trophîme. Western façade, northern end. Samson. L. W. P. phot.

1369. ARLES, (Bouches-du-Rhône), St.-Trophîme. Western façade, southern portion. Part of Last Judgment; Annunciation; Annunciation to Zacharias; Magi; St. Peter; St. John, St. Trophîme, St. James, St. Bartholomew. F. M. S. phot.

1370. ARLES, (Bouches-du-Rhône), St.-Trophîme. Western portal, detail of northern impost. The three Patriarchs; two Apostles; Slaughter of the Innocents; Annunciation to Zacharias; Annunciation. F. M. S. phot. from cast.

1371. ARLES, (Bouches-du-Rhône), St.-Trophîme. Western portal, northern jamb. St. Peter, St. John. Stoedtner phot.

1372. ARLES, (Bouches-du-Rhône), St.-Trophîme. Tympanum of western portal. *Majestas Domini.* A. K. P. phot.

1373. ARLES, (Bouches-du-Rhône), St.-Trophîme. Western portal, southern jamb. St. Paul, St. Andrew. L. W. P. phot.

1374. ARLES, (Bouches-du-Rhône), St.-Trophîme. Western façade, southern jamb. Story of the Magi; St. Paul, St. Andrew; Passion of St. Stephen. L. W. P. phot.

1375. ARLES, (Bouches-du-Rhône), St.-Trophîme. Western façade, southern frieze. The Damned. L. W. P. phot.

1376. ARLES, (Bouches-du-Rhône), St.-Trophîme. Western façade, southern end. St. James, St. Philip. L. W. P. phot.

1377. ARLES, (Bouches-du-Rhône), St.-Trophîme. Western façade, southern end. Hell. L. W. P. phot.

1378. NÎMES, (Gard), Cathédrale. Frieze of western façade. Temptation; Shame; God walks in Garden; Expulsion. A. K. P. phot.

1379. NÎMES, (Gard), Cathédrale. Frieze of western façade. Expulsion, Offerings of Cain and Abel, Murder of Abel, Noah's Ark. A. K. P. phot.

1380. NÎMES, (Gard), Cathédrale. Detail of frieze, western façade. Adam, from the Temptation. A. K. P. phot.

1381. NÎMES, (Gard), Cathédrale. Detail of frieze, western façade. Eve, from the Temptation. A. K. P. phot. from cast.

1382. NÎMES, (Gard), Cathédrale. Frieze of western façade, detail. God in the Garden. A. K. P. phot. from cast.

1383. NÎMES, (Gard), Cathédrale. Frieze of western façade, detail. Offering of Cain. A. K. P. phot. from cast.

1384. MAGUELONNE, (Hérault). Portal of south transept, tympanum. *Majestas Domini*. 1178. L. W. P. phot.

1385. ST.-GILLES, (Gard). Western façade, tympanum of southern portal. The Crucifixion. A. K. P. phot.

1386. ST.-GILLES, (Gard). Western façade, tympanum of northern portal. The Adoration of the Magi. A. K. P. phot.

1387. ST.-GILLES, (Gard). Detail of frieze, north of northern portal. Preparation for the Entry into Jerusalem. Stoedtner phot.

1388. ST.-GILLES, (Gard). Lintel of northern portal. Detail of Entry into Jerusalem. Stoedtner phot.

1389. ST.-GILLES, (Gard). Lintel of northern portal. Detail of Entry into Jerusalem. Stoedtner phot.

1390. ST.-GILLES, (Gard). Detail of frieze, north of southern portal. The Magdalen anoints Christ's Feet. Stoedtner phot.

1391. ST.-GILLES, (Gard). Western façade, tympanum and lintel of southern portal. The Crucifixion; the Maries buy Spices; the Maries at the Tomb. Stoedtner phot.

1392. ST.-GILLES, (Gard). Western façade, northern end. St. Michael and the Dragon. A. K. P. phot.

1393. ST.-GILLES, (Gard). Western façade, northern end. Detail of St. Michael. Stoedtner phot.

1394.   St.-Gilles, (Gard). Western façade, southern end. Fall of the rebellious Angels. A. K. P. phot.

1395.   St.-Gilles, (Gard). Western façade, southern end. Detail of Fall of the rebellious Angels. Stoedtner phot.

1396.   St.-Gilles, (Gard). Western façade, southern end. Detail of Fall of the rebellious Angels. Stoedtner phot.

1397.   St.-Guilhem-le-Désert (?), (Hérault). Fragments now in court of University, Montpellier. Christ and Apostles. A. K. P. phot.

1398.   St.-Guilhem-le-Désert (?), (Hérault). Fragments now in court of University, Montpellier. Apostles. A. K. P. phot.

1399.   St.-Guilhem-le-Désert (?), (Hérault). Fragment now in church. Two Apostles (?). L. W. P. phot.

1400.   St.-Guilhem-le-Désert (?), (Hérault). Fragments now in Musée Archéologique, Montpellier. Two Elders. A. K. P. phot.

1401.   St.-Guilhem-le-Désert (?), (Hérault). Fragments now in Musée Archéologique, Montpellier. Two Elders. A. K. P. phot.

1402.   St.-Guilhem-le-Désert (?), (Hérault). Fragments now in Musée Archéologique, Montpellier. Two Elders. (Heads restored.) A. K. P. phot.

1403.   St.-Guilhem-le-Désert (?), (Hérault). Capital now in collection of Mr. Raymond Pitcairn, Bryn Athyn, Penn.

1404.   Rieux-Minervois, (Aude). Capital of interior. The Ravishing of the Magdalen. L. W. P. phot.

1404 a. Tarascon, (Bouches-du-Rhône), Ste.-Marthe. Console east of south portal. L. W. P. phot.

1404 b. Tarascon, (Bouches-du-Rhône), Ste.-Marthe. Console west of south portal. L. W. P. phot.

1405.   Salon, (Bouches-du-Rhône), St.-Michel. Tympanum of western portal. St. Michael; the Lamb of God. L. W. P. phot.

1406.   Aix-en-Provence, (Bouches-du-Rhône), Cathédrale. Cloister, north-west angle. An Angel. L. W. P. phot.

1407.   Aix-en-Provence, (Bouches-du-Rhône), Cathédrale. Cloister, east gallery. L. W. P. phot.

1408.   Aix-en-Provence, (Bouches-du-Rhône), Cathédrale. Cloister, east gallery, sculptured column. A. K. P. phot.

1409.   Marseille, (Bouches-du-Rhône), Musée Borély. Capital said to come from Montmajour. The Feast at Emmaus. A. K. P. phot.

1410.   Marseille, (Bouches-du-Rhône), Musée Borély. Fragment of a pulpit. St. John the Evangelist. A. K. P. phot.

1278. Marseille, (Bouches-du-Rhône), St.-Victor. Tomb of St. Isarne, † 1048,
now in museum. Giraudon phot. from cast.

1279. REGENSBURG, (Bavaria), St.-Emmeran. Relief now south of western portal.
Christ. 1049-1064. Stoedtner phot.

1280. REGENSBURG, (Bavaria), St.-Emmeran. Relief now south of western portal.
Christ. 1049-1064. Stoedtner phot.

1281. REGENSBURG, (Bavaria), St.-Emmeran. Relief now flanking western portals.
St. Emmeran. Stoedtner phot.

1282. REGENSBURG, (Bavaria), St.-Emmeran. Relief now flanking western portals.
St. Dionysus. Stoedtner phot.

1283. MARSEILLE, (Bouches-du-Rhône), Cathédrale Ancienne. Altar-frontal, detail. St. Cannate. 1122. A. K. P. phot.

1285. MAGUELONNE, (Hérault), Cathédrale. Southern transept, western portal, northern corbel. St. Peter. A. K. P. phot.

1286. MAGUELONNE, (Hérault), Cathédrale. Southern transept, western portal, southern corbel. St. Paul. A. K. P. phot.

1287. MAGUELONNE, (Hérault), Cathédrale. Relief south of western portal,
southern transept. St. Peter. A. K. P. phot. from cast.

1288. Maguelonne, (Hérault), Cathédrale. Relief north of western portal, southern transept. St. Paul. L. W. P. phot.

1280. ST.-HILAIRE, (Aude). Tombeau de St. Hilaire. St. Hilaire is arrested.

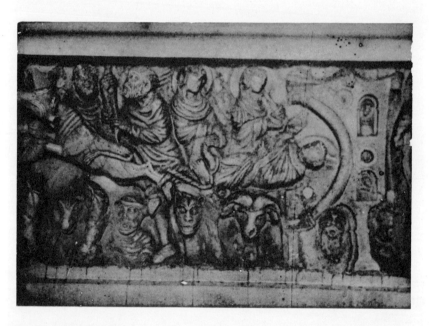

1290. ST.-HILAIRE, (Aude). Tombeau de St. Hilaire. Martyrdom of St. Saturnin.
       A. K. P. phot.

1291. St.-Gabriel, (Bouches-du-Rhône). Relief of western façade. The Annun-

1292. BEAUCAIRE, (Gard), Notre-Dame-des-Pommiers. Frieze now in southern façade. Washing the Feet; Last Supper; Judas receives the Price of his Treason; Executioners. A. K. P. phot.

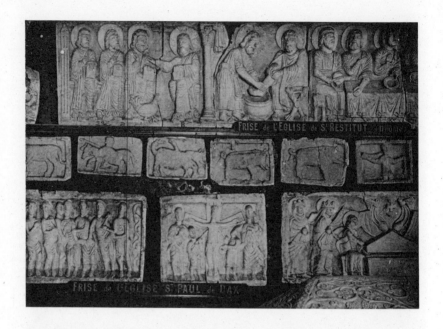

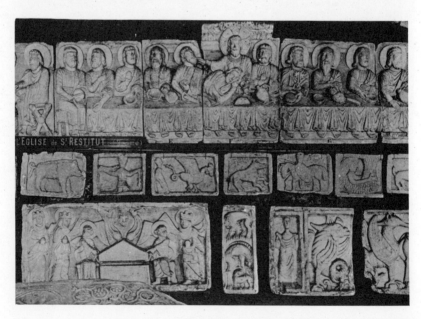

1293. BEAUCAIRE, (Gard), Notre-Dame-des-Pommiers. Frieze now in southern
façade, detail. Peter denies Christ; Washing the Feet, Last Supper.
A. K. P. phot. from cast.

1294. BEAUCAIRE, (Gard), Notre-Dame-des-Pommiers. Frieze now in southern
façade, detail. Last Supper. A. K. P. phot. from cast.

1295. BEAUCAIRE, (Gard), Notre-Dame-des-Pommiers. Frieze now in southern
    façade, detail. Last Supper, Judas receives the Price of his Treason,
    Betrayal. A. K. P. phot. from cast.

1296. BEAUCAIRE, (Gard), Notre-Dame-des-Pommiers. Frieze now in southern
    façade, detail. Betrayal, Christ before Pilate, Flagellation. A. K. P.
    phot. from cast.

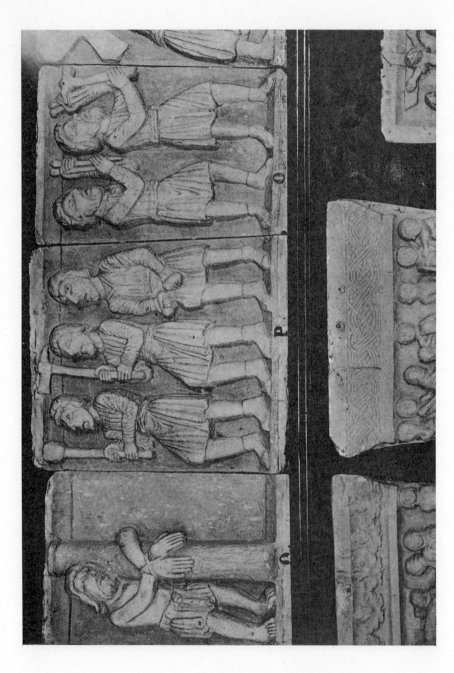

1297. BEAUCAIRE, (Gard), Notre-Dame-des-Pommiers. Frieze now in southern

1298. BEAUCAIRE, (Gard), Notre-Dame-des-Pommiers. Frieze now in southern
façade, detail. Carrying the Cross; the Maries buying Spices; the Maries
at the Tomb. A. K. P. phot. from cast.

1299.   BEAUCAIRE, (Gard), Notre-Dame-des-Pommiers. Virgin of the Adoration, from tympanum, now in house of priest. L. W. P. phot.

1300. St.-Guilhem-le-Désert, (Hérault). Altar-frontal. *Majestas Domini*, Crucifixion. L. W. P. phot.

1301. FONTFROIDE, (Aude). Relief now in court of university. Montpellier.
Adoration of the Magi. A. K. P. phot.

1302. ST.-GILLES, (Gard). Western façade, statue south of northern portal. St. Matthew. Signed by Brunus. A. K. P. phot.

1303.   St.-Gilles, (Gard). Western façade, second statue south of northern portal.
St. Bartholomew. A. K. P. phot.

1304. St.-Gilles, (Gard). Western façade, second statue north of central portal. St. Thomas. A. K. P. phot.

1305. St.-Gilles, (Gard). Western façade, relief north of central portal. St. James the Less. A. K. P. phot.

1306. St.-Gilles, (Gard). Northern jamb of central portal, western façade. Detail of St. John. A. K. P. phot.

1307. ST.-GILLES, (Gard). Northern jamb of central portal, western façade. Detail of St. John. A. K. P. phot.

1308. St.-Gilles, (Gard). Northern jamb of central portal, western façade. Detail of St. Peter. A. K. P. phot.

1309. ST.-GILLES, (Gard). Northern jamb of central portal, western façade. Detail of St. Peter. A. K. P. phot.

1310. St.-Gilles, (Gard). Western façade, southern jamb of central portal.
Detail of St. James the Less. A. K. P. phot.

1311. St.-Gilles, (Gard). Western façade, southern jamb of central portal. Detail of St. Paul. A. K. P. phot.

1312. ST.-GILLES, (Gard). Western façade, reliefs south of central portal. Two
Apostles.

1313. ST.-GILLES, (Gard). Western façade, relief south of central portal, detail. An Apostle. Stoedtner phot.

1314. ST.-GILLES, (Gard). Western façade, statues north of southern portal. Two
Apostles. A. K. P. phot.

1315. St.-Gilles, (Gard). Western façade, frieze north of central portal. The Money-Changers; they are driven from the Temple; Martha and Mary supplicate Christ; Raising of Lazarus; St. Bartholomew, St. Thomas, St. James the Less. Giraudon phot. from cast.

1316. St.-Gilles, (Gard). Western façade, frieze north of central portal. The Money-Changers; they are driven from the Temple; Martha and Mary supplicate Christ; Raising of Lazarus. F. M. S. phot. from cast.

1317. St.-Gilles, (Gard). Western façade, frieze north of central portal. The Money-Changers driven from the Temple; Martha and Mary supplicate

1318. St.-Gilles, (Gard). Western façade, lintel of central portal. The Last Supper. A. K. P. phot.

1319.   ST.-GILLES, (Gard).   Western façade, frieze in reveal south of central portal.
          Detail of the Betrayal.   Stoedtner phot.
1320.   ST.-GILLES, (Gard).   Western façade, frieze in reveal south of central portal.
          Detail of the Betrayal.   A. K. P. phot. from cast.

1321. St.-Gilles, (Gard). Western façade, frieze south of central portal. Christ before Pilate; the Flagellation. F. M. S. phot.

1322. St.-Gilles, (Gard). Western façade, frieze south of central portal. Pilate;
the Flagellation. Girardon phot. from cast.

1323. St.-Gilles, (Gard), Abbaye. Detail of architrave south of central portal. Stoedtner phot.

1324. ST.-GILLES, (Gard). Western façade, socle north of central portal. The
Murder of Abel. Stoedtner phot.

1325. St.-Gilles, (Gard). Western façade, socle north of central portal. The Sacrifices of Cain and Abel. A. K. P. phot.

1325 a. St.-Gilles, (Gard). Western facade, podium north of central portal. F. M. S. phot. from cast.

1325 b. St.-Gilles, (Gard). Western façade, podium south of central portal.
F. M. S. phot. from cast.

1226. St.-Gilles. (Gard). Western façade, socle south of central portal. David

1327. ST.-GILLES, (Gard). Western façade, socle south of central portal. The
Angel of the Lord appears to David; Samson. A. K. P. phot.

1328. St.-Gilles, (Gard). Western façade, socle south of central portal. A. K. P. phot.

1329. St.-Gilles, (Gard). Fragment now in ruins of choir. Adoration of the Magi. A. K. P. phot.

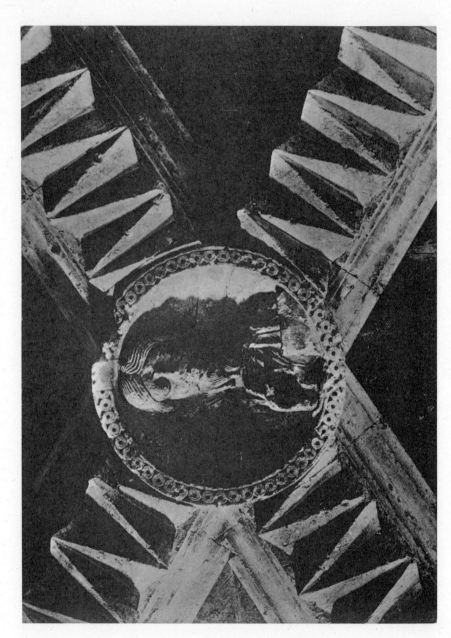

1331. Aix-en-Provence, (Bouches-du-Rhône), Cathédrale. Relief in choir.
A. K. P. phot.

1332. MONTMAJOUR, (Bouches-du-Rhône). Relief west of portal in cloister.
L. W. P. phot.

1333. MONTMAJOUR, (Bouches-du-Rhône). Relief east of portal in cloister.
L. W. P. phot.

1334. ROMANS, (Drôme), St.-Barnard. Western portal, northern jamb. St. Peter, St. James. B.-A. phot.

1335. ROMANS, (Drôme), St.-Barnard. Western portal, southern jamb. St. John, St. Paul. L. W. P. phot.

1336. ROMANS, (Drôme), St.-Barnard. Capital of western portal. The Journey to Emmaus. L. W. P. phot.

1337. Romans, (Drôme), St.-Barnard. Western portal, capital. L. W. P. phot.
1338. Romans, (Drôme), St.-Barnard. Capital of nave. The Annunciation.
L. W. P. phot.

1339. AVIGNON, (Vaucluse), Notre-Dame-des-Doms. Episcopal throne composed with ancient fragments. St. Mark. Silvestre phot.

1340.   AVIGNON, (Vaucluse), Notre-Dame-des-Doms. Episcopal throne composed
of ancient fragments. St. Luke. Silvestre phot.

1341. AVIGNON, (Vaucluse). Musée Calvet. Capital. Job. Silvestre phot.

1342. AVIGNON, (Vaucluse), Notre-Dame-des-Doms. Capital of cloister, now in
Fogg Museum, Cambridge, Mass. Samson and the Lion. F. M. phot.

1343.   Avignon, (Vaucluse), Notre-Dame-des-Doms. Capital of cloister, now in
Fogg Museum, Cambridge, Mass. Delilah cuts Samson's Hair. F. M.
phot.

1344. ARLES, (Bouches-du-Rhône), St.-Trophîme. North-west pier of cloister. St. John. L. W. P. phot.

1345. ARLES, (Bouches-du-Rhône), St.-Trophîme. North-west pier of cloister. St. Trophîme. F. M. S. phot. from cast.

1346. ARLES, (Bouches-du-Rhône), St.-Trophime. Detail of north-west pier of cloister. St. Trophime. Stoedtner phot.

1347. ARLES, (Bouches-du-Rhône), St.-Trophîme. North-west pier of cloister. St. Peter. A. K. P. phot.

1348. ARLES, (Bouches-du-Rhône), St.-Trophîme. Detail of north-west pier of
cloister. Detail of St. Peter. Stoedtner phot.

1349. ARLES, (Bouches-du-Rhône), St.-Trophîme. Northern gallery of cloister, first pier. St. James, a Pilgrim. L. W. P. phot.

1350. ARLES, (Bouches-du-Rhône), St.-Trophîme. Northern gallery of cloister,
first pier. St. James, a Pilgrim. A. K. P. phot.

1351. ARLES, (Bouches-du-Rhône), St.-Trophîme. Northern gallery of cloister,

1352. ARLES, (Bouches-du-Rhône), St.-Trophîme. Northern gallery of cloister, second pier. St. James the Less. A. K. P. phot.

1353. ARLES, (Bouches-du-Rhône), St.-Trophîme. North-east pier of cloister.
St. Paul, the Ascension, St. Stephen. L. W. P. phot.

1354. ARLES, (Bouches-du-Rhône), St.-Trophîme. North-east pier of cloister. St. Stephen. A. K. P. phot.

1355. ARLES, (Bouches-du-Rhône), St.-Trophîme. North-east pier of cloister. St. Matthew; Passion of St. Stephen. A. K. P. phot.

1356. ARLES, (Bouches-du-Rhône), St.-Trophîme. North-east pier of cloister.
St. Stephen, Passion of St. Stephen, St. Matthew. L. W. P. phot.

1357. ARLES, (Bouches-du-Rhône), St.-Trophtme. Eastern gallery of cloister, first pier. Judas (?). A. K. P. phot.

1358. ARLES, (Bouches-du-Rhône), St.-Trophtme. Eastern gallery of cloister, second pier. The Queen of Sheba. A. K. P. phot.

1359. ARLES, (Bouches-du-Rhône), St.-Trophîme. Eastern gallery of cloister, second pier. Solomon. L. W. P. phot.

1360. ARLES, (Bouches-du-Rhône), St.-Trophîme. Capital of east gallery of cloister. Entry into Jerusalem; Conversion of St. Paul. A. K. P. phot.

1361. ARLES, (Bouches-du-Rhône), St.-Trophîme. Reliefs of south-east pier of cloister. Washing the Feet, Last Supper, Betrayal. A. K. P. phot.

1363. ARLES, (Bouches-du-Rhône), St.-Trophîme. Holy-water basin at south-
      east angle of cloister. L. W. P. phot.

1364.   ARLES, (Bouches-du-Rhône), St.-Trophîme. Holy-water basin at south-east angle of cloister. A. K. P. phot.

1366. Arles, (Bouches-du-Rhône), St.-Trophime. Western façade. The Last
Judgment. B.-A. phot.

1367. ARLES, (Bouches-du-Rhône), St.-Trophîme. Western façade, northern end. The Temptation; Psychostasy. L. W. P. phot.

1368. ARLES, (Bouches-du-Rhône), St.-Trophîme. Western façade, northern end.
Samson. L. W. P. phot.

1369. ARLES, (Bouches-du-Rhône), St.-Trophîme. Western façade, southern portion. Part of Last Judgment; Annunciation; Annunciation to Zacharias; Mari: St. Peter: St. Iohn, St. Trophîme, St. James, St.

1370. ARLES, (Bouches-du-Rhône), St.-Trophîme. Western portal, detail of
northern impost. The three Patriarchs; two Apostles; Slaughter of the
Innocents; Annunciation to Zacharias; Annunciation. F. M. S. phot.
from cast.

1371. ARLES, (Bouches-du-Rhône), St.-Trophîme. Western portal, northern jamb. St. Peter, St. John. Stoedtner phot.

1372. ARLES, (Bouches-du-Rhône), St.-Trophtme. Tympanum of western portal.
Majestas Domini. A. K. P. phot.

1373. ARLES, (Bouches-du-Rhône), St.-Trophîme. Western portal, southern
jamb. St. Paul, St. Andrew. L. W. P. phot.

1374. ARLES, (Bouches-du-Rhône), St.-Trophîme. Western façade, southern
jamb. Story of the Magi; St. Paul, St. Andrew; Passion of St. Stephen.
L. W. P. phot.

1375. ARLES, (Bouches-du-Rhône), St.-Trophîme. Western façade, southern frieze. The Damned. L. W. P. phot.

1376. ARLES, (Bouches-du-Rhône), St.-Trophîme. Western façade, southern
end. St. James, St. Philip. L. W. P. phot.

1377. ARLES, (Bouches-du-Rhône), St.-Trophîme. Western façade, southern end.
Hell. L. W. P. phot.

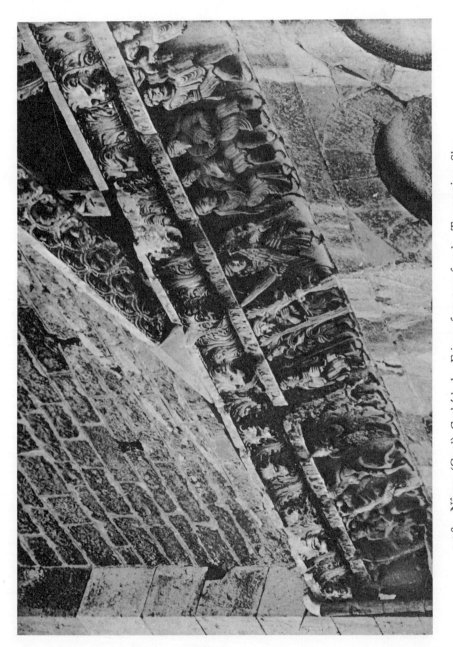

1378. Nîmes, (Gard), Cathédrale. Frieze of western façade. Temptation; Shame; God walks in Garden; Expulsion. A. K. P. phot.

1379.   Nîmes, (Gard), Cathédrale.   Frieze of western façade.   Expulsion, Offerings

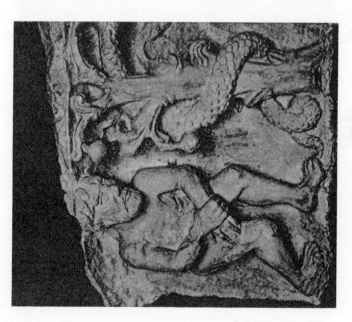

1380. Nîmes, (Gard), Cathédrale. Detail of frieze, western façade. Adam, from the Temptation. A. K. P. phot.

1381. Nîmes, (Gard), Cathédrale. Detail of frieze, western façade. Eve, from the Temptation. A. K. P. phot. from cast.

1382. NÎMES, (Gard), Cathédrale. Frieze of western façade, detail. God in the
Garden. A. K. P. phot. from cast.

1383. NÎMES, (Gard), Cathédrale. Frieze of western façade, detail. Offering of

1384. MAGUELONNE, (Hérault). Portal of south transept, tympanum. *Majestas Domini.* 1178. L. W. P. phot.

1385. St.-Gilles, (Gard). Western façade, tympanum of southern portal. The Crucifixion. A. K. P. phot.

1386. St.-Gilles, (Gard). Western façade, tympanum of northern portal. The Adoration of the Magi. A. K. P. phot.

1387. St.-Gilles, (Gard). Detail of frieze, north of northern portal. Preparation for the Entry into Jerusalem. Stoedtner phot.

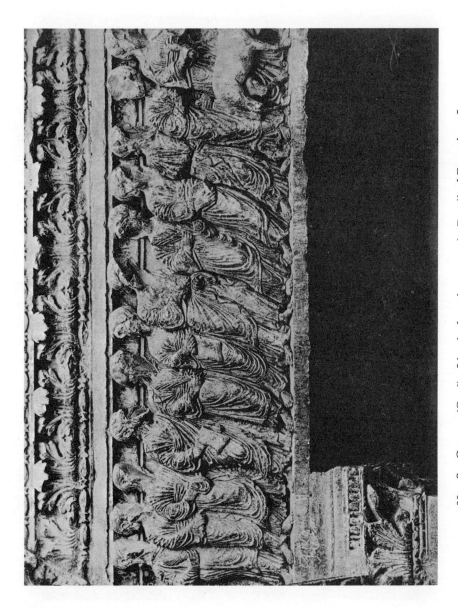

1388.   St.-Gilles, (Gard).   Lintel of northern portal.   Detail of Entry into Jerusalem.   Stoedtner phot.

1389. St.-Gilles, (Gard). Lintel of northern portal. Detail of Entry into Jerusalem. Stoedtner phot.

1390. St.-Gilles, (Gard). Detail of frieze, north of southern portal. The Magdalen anoints Christ's Feet. Stoedtner phot.

1391. ST.-GILLES, (Gard). Western façade, tympanum and lintel of southern portal. The Crucifixion; the Maries buy Spices; the Maries at the Tomb.

1392. St.-Gilles, (Gard). Western façade, northern end. St. Michael and the Dragon. A. K. P. phot.

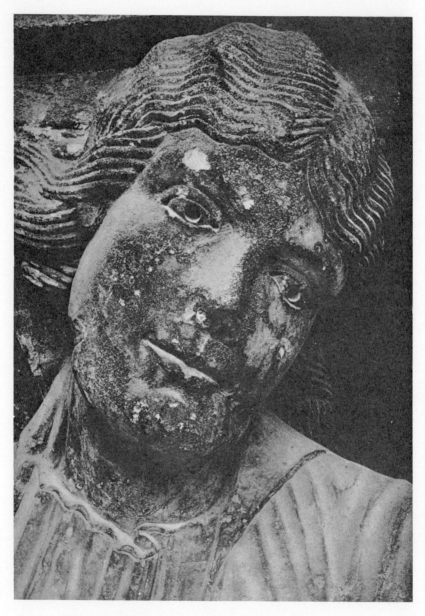

1393. St.-Gilles, (Gard). Western façade, northern end. Detail of St. Michael. Stoedtner phot.

1394. ST.-GILLES, (Gard). Western façade, southern end. Fall of the rebellious
Angels. A. K. P. phot.

1395. St.-Gilles, (Gard). Western façade, southern end. Detail of Fall of the rebellious Angels. Stoedtner phot.

1396. St.-Gilles, (Gard). Western façade, southern end. Detail of Fall of the rebellious Angels. Stoedtner phot.

1397. St.-Guilhem-le-Désert (?), (Hérault). Fragments now in court of University, Montpellier. Christ and Apostles. A. K. P. phot.

1398.   St.-Guilhem-le-Désert (?), (Hérault). Fragments now in court of University, Montpellier. Apostles. A. K. P. phot.

1399. St.-Guilhem-le-Désert (?), (Hérault). Fragment now in church. Two Apostles (?). L. W. P. phot.

1400. St.-Guilhem-le-Désert (?), (Hérault). Fragments now in Musée Archéologique, Montpellier. Two Elders. A. K. P. phot.

1401. ST.-GUILHEM-LE-DÉSERT (?), (Hérault). Fragments now in Musée Archéologique, Montpellier. Two Elders. A. K. P. phot.

1402.   St.-Guilhem-le-Désert (?), (Hérault). Fragments now in Musée Archéologique, Montpellier. Two Elders. (Heads restored.) A. K. P. phot.

1403. St.-Guilhem-le-Désert (?), (Hérault). Capital now in collection of Mr. Raymond Pitcairn, Bryn Athyn, Penn.

1404. Rieux-Minervois, (Aude). Capital of interior. The Ravishing of the Magdalen. L. W. P. phot.

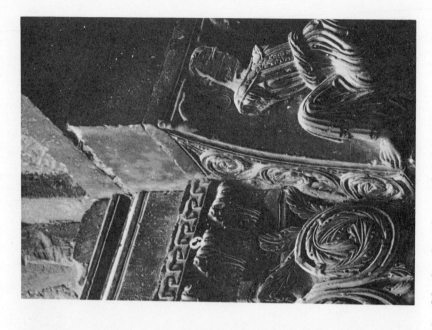

1404 a. TARASCON, (Bouches-du-Rhône), Ste.-Marthe. Console east of south portal.
L. W. P. phot.

1404 b. TARASCON, (Bouches-du-Rhône), Ste.-Marthe. Console west of south

1405. SALON, (Bouches-du-Rhône), St.-Michel. Tympanum of western portal.
St. Michael; the Lamb of God. L. W. P. phot.

1406. AIX-EN-PROVENCE, (Bouches-du-Rhône), Cathédrale. Cloister, north-west ·
angle. An Angel. L. W. P. phot.

1407. Aix-en-Provence, (Bouches-du-Rhône), Cathédrale. Cloister, east gallery.
L. W. P. phot.

1408. AIX-EN-PROVENCE, (Bouches-du-Rhône), Cathédrale. Cloister, east gallery,
sculptured column. A. K. P. phot.

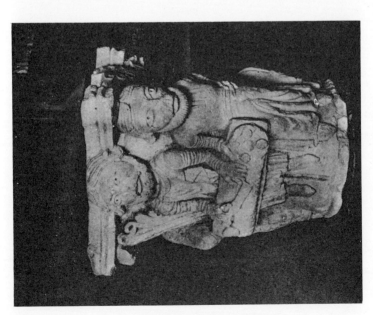

1409.   MARSEILLE, (Bouches-du-Rhône), Musée Borély. Capital said to come from
        Montmajour. The Feast at Emmaus. A. K. P. phot.

1410.   MARSEILLE, (Bouches-du-Rhône), Musée Borély. Fragment of a pulpit.
        St. John the Evangelist. A. K. P. phot.

ROMANESQUE SCULPTURE

OF THE PILGRIMAGE ROADS

VOLUME X

ILE-DE-FRANCE

ILLUSTRATIONS

ILLUSTRATIONS

(1411–1527)

ILE-DE-FRANCE

1411. BEAUVAIS, (Oise), Basse-Oeuvre. Western portal, detail. Stoedtner phot.

1412. LE MANS, (Sarthe), La Couture. Relief in northern wall. Christ. A. K. P. phot.

1413. ETAMPES, (Seine-et-Oise), St.-Basile. Archivolts of western portal. The Last Judgment. L. W. P. phot.

1414. ST.-BENOÎT-SUR-LOIRE, (Loiret). Capital of narthex. Seven Martyrs. L. W. P. phot.

1415. ST.-BENO T-SUR-LOIRE, (Loiret). Capital of narthex. Apotheosis of St. Martin. L. W. P. phot.

1416. ST.-BENOÎT-SUR-LOIRE, (Loiret). Capital of narthex. Annunciation; Infant Christ and St. Joseph; Visitation; Christ in Temple. L. W. P. phot.

1417. ST.-BENOÎT-SUR-LOIRE, (Loiret). Capital of narthex. Scenes from the Apocalypse. L. W. P. phot.

1418. ST.-BENOÎT-SUR-LOIRE, (Loiret). Capital of choir. A. K. P. phot.

1419. ST.-BENOÎT-SUR-LOIRE, (Loiret). Capital of narthex. The Horsemen of the Apocalypse. L. W. P. phot.

1420. ST.-BENOÎT-SUR-LOIRE, (Loiret). Capital of triforium. St. Benedict, Hugh, the Virgin. Giraudon phot. from cast.

1421. ST.-BENOÎT-SUR-LOIRE, (Loiret). Fragments of altar-frontal. St. James. A. K. P. phot.

1422. ST.-BENOÎT-SUR-LOIRE, (Loiret). Fragments of altar-frontal. St. James, an Apostle. A. K. P. phot.

1423. BEAUVAIS, (Oise), St.-Etienne. Northern transept, detail of rose. The Wheel of Fortune. F. M. S. phot.

1424. BEAUVAIS, (Oise), St.-Etienne. Northern transept, detail of rose. The Wheel of Fortune. F. M. S. phot.

1425. CHÂTEAUDUN, (Eure-et-Loir), La Madeleine. Northern façade, according to the drawing made for Montfaucon. B.-A. phot.

1426. CHÂTEAUDUN, (Eure-et-Loir), La Madeleine. Sculptures of northern façade, according to a drawing made for Montfaucon. B.-A. phot.

1427. CHÂTEAUDUN, (Eure-et-Loir), La Madeleine. Sculptures of northern façade, according to a drawing made for Montfaucon. B.-A. phot.

1428. CHÂTEAUDUN, (Eure-et-Loir), La Madeleine. Southern portal, archivolt. L. W. P. phot.

1429. CHÂTEAUDUN, (Eure-et-Loir), La Madeleine. Southern portal, detail of voussures. L. W. P. phot.

1430. CHÂTEAUDUN, (Eure-et-Loir), La Madeleine. Southern portal, detail of voussures. L. W. P. phot.

1431. ST.-QUENTIN-LÈS-BEAUVAIS, (Oise). Sculptured colonnette now in Beauvais museum. A. K. P. phot.

1432. ST.-QUENTIN-LÈS-BEAUVAIS, (Oise). Sculptured colonnette now in Beauvais museum. A. K. P. phot.

1433 ST.-QUENTIN-LÈS-BEAUVAIS, (Oise). Sculptured colonnette now in Beauvais museum. A. K. P. phot.

1434. BRIARE, (Loiret). Fragment of altar-frontal now in Musée Historique, Orléans. L. W. P. phot.

1435. ST.-DENIS, (Seine), Abbaye. Capital of crypt. F. M. S. phot.

1436. ST.-DENIS, (Seine), Abbaye. Capital of crypt. F. M. S. phot.

1437. ST.-DENIS, (Seine), Abbaye. Western façade, northern portal. Detail of voussures. Moses, David. L. W. P. phot.

1438. ST.-DENIS, (Seine), Abbaye. Western façade, northern portal, detail of socle. Aquarius. L. W. P. phot.

1439. ST.-DENIS, (Seine), Abbaye. Western façade, detail of central portal. The Last Judgment. L. W. P. phot.

1440. ST.-DENIS, (Seine), Abbaye. Western façade, central portal, northern voussures. The Elders, the Last Judgment. F. M. S. phot.

1441. ST.-DENIS, (Seine), Abbaye. Western façade, central portal, northern jamb. A foolish Virgin. F. M. S. phot.

1442. ST.-DENIS, (Seine), Abbaye. Western façade, central portal, southern jamb. A wise Virgin. L. W. P. phot.

1443. ST.-DENIS, (Seine), Abbaye. Western façade, southern portal, northern jamb. November and December. F. M. S. phot.

1444. ST.-DENIS, (Seine), Abbaye. Western façade, southern portal, southern jamb. February and January. F. M. S. phot.

1445. ST.-DENIS, (Seine), Abbaye. Destroyed sculptures of west façade, southern portal, from Montfaucon's drawings. Moses and a Prophet. B.-A. phot.

1446. ST.-DENIS, (Seine), Abbaye. Destroyed jamb sculpture of western façade, from Montfaucon's drawing. B.-A. phot.

1447. ST.-DENIS, (Seine), Abbaye. Destroyed jamb sculpture of western façade, from Montfaucon's drawing. B.-A. phot.

1448. ST.-DENIS, (Seine), Abbaye. Destroyed jamb sculpture of western façade, from Montfaucon's drawing. B.-A. phot.

1449. ST.-DENIS, (Seine), Abbaye. Destroyed jamb sculpture of western façade, from Montfaucon's drawing. B.-A. phot.

1450. ST.-DENIS, (Seine), Abbaye. Destroyed jamb sculpture of western façade, from Montfaucon's drawing. B.-A. phot.

1451. ST.-DENIS, (Seine), Abbaye. Destroyed jamb sculpture of western façade, from Montfaucon's drawing. B.-A. phot.

1452. St.-Denis, (Seine), Abbaye. Destroyed jamb sculpture of western façade, from Montfaucon's drawing. B.-A. phot.

1453. St.-Denis, (Seine), Abbaye. Destroyed jamb sculpture of western façade, from Montfaucon's drawing. B.-A. phot.

1454. St.-Denis, (Seine), Abbaye. Western façade, northern portal, destroyed jamb figure, from Montfaucon's drawing. B.-A. phot.

1455. St.-Denis, (Seine), Abbaye. Destroyed jamb sculpture of western façade, from Montfaucon's drawing. B.-A. phot.

1456. St.-Denis, (Seine), Abbaye. Destroyed jamb sculpture of western façade, from Montfaucon's drawing. B.-A. phot.

1457. St.-Denis, (Seine), Abbaye. Destroyed jamb sculptures of western façade, from Montfaucon's drawing. B.-A. phot.

1458. Paris, Musée du Louvre. Heads. Giraudon phot.

1459. Paris, Musée du Louvre. Heads. Giraudon phot.

1460. Etampes, (Seine-et-Oise), Notre-Dame. Southern portal. Angels, Prophets, Elders; Ascension; Birth of Christ; Precursors of Christ. L. W. P. phot.

1461. Etampes, (Seine-et-Oise), Notre-Dame. Southern portal, western spandrel. A Prophet, an Angel; Prophets, Elders. L. W. P. phot.

1462. Etampes, (Seine-et-Oise), Notre-Dame. Tympanum of southern portal. Prophets, Elders, Ascension. B.-A. phot.

1463. Etampes, (Seine-et-Oise), Notre-Dame. Southern portal, western jamb. Esther, Moses, Melchisedek. B.-A. phot.

1464. Etampes, (Seine-et-Oise), Notre-Dame. Southern portal, eastern jamb. David, Solomon, the Queen of Sheba. B.-A. phot.

1465. Etampes, (Seine-et-Oise), Notre-Dame. Statue now in chapel. St. Peter. B.-A. phot.

1466. Etampes, (Seine-et-Oise), Notre-Dame. Statue now in chapel. St. Paul. B.-A. phot.

1467. Corbeil, (Seine-et-Oise), Notre-Dame. Jamb sculpture now in Louvre. The Queen of Sheba. Restored. Stoedtner phot.

1468. Corbeil, (Seine-et-Oise), Notre-Dame. Jamb sculpture, now in Louvre. Solomon. Restored. Stoedtner phot.

1469. La Celle Bruère, (Cher). Relief of façade. L. W. P. phot.

1470. La Celle Bruère, (Cher). Relief of façade. L. W. P. phot.

1471. Coulombs, (Eure-et-Loir). Sculptured column now in Louvre. The Sleep of the Magi. F. M. S. phot.

1472. Coulombs, (Eure-et-Loir). Sculptured column now in Louvre. F. M. S. phot.

1473. Coulombs, (Eure-et-Loir). Sculptured column now in Louvre. F. M. S. phot.

1474. Ivry-la-Bataille, (Eure), Abbaye. Western portal. Patriarchs, Angels, Elders, Virtues. L. W. P. phot.

1475. Ivry-la-Bataille, (Eure), Abbaye. Western portal, detail of voussures. Angels. L. W. P. phot.

1476. Ivry-la-Bataile, (Eure), Abbaye. Western portal, detail of voussures. Elders, Angels. L. W. P. phot.

1477. Ivry-la-Bataille, (Eure), Abbaye. Western portal. Detail of voussures. L. W. P. phot.

1478. Ivry-la-Bataille, (Eure), Abbaye. Western portal, southern jamb. The Queen of Sheba. L. W. P. phot.

1479. Véreaux, (Cher). Southern jamb of western portal. L. W. P. phot.

1480. Véreaux, (Cher). Northern jamb of western portal. L. W. P. phot.

1481. Véreaux, (Cher). Southern jamb of western portal, detail. L. W. P. phot.

1482. Mervilliers, (Eure-et-Loir). Tympanum of southern portal. A Knight doing Fealty to St. Poragie. L. W. P. phot.

1483. Mervilliers, (Eure-et-Loir). Tympanum of southern portal. A Knight doing Fealty to St. Poragie. L. W. P. phot.

1484. Paris, Musée du Louvre. Virgin in wood. Giraudon phot.

1485. Carrière-St.-Denis, (Seine-et-Oise). Altar-frontal now in Louvre. Annunciation; Virgin; Baptism. Giraudon phot.

1486. Carrière-St.-Denis, (Seine-et-Oise). Altar-frontal, now in Louvre, detail. The Virgin. Giraudon phot.

1487. Châlons-sur-Marne, (Marne), Notre-Dame. Fragment of pier, now in Louvre. Crusaders. B.-A. phot.

1488. Paris, Ste. Geneviève. Capital now in Louvre. Daniel and the Lions. F. M. S. phot.

1489. Issy, (Seine). Relief now in garden of priest's house. *Majestas Domini.* L. W. P. phot.

1490. Provins, (Seine-et-Marne), St.-Ayoul. Western portal, tympanum and voussures. Angels, Elders, Seraphim, the Blessed, the Damned; *Majestas Domini.* L. W. P. phot.

1491. Provins, (Seine-et-Marne), St.-Ayoul. Western portal, southern jamb. L. W. P. phot.

1492. St.-Loup-de-Naud, (Seine-et-Marne). Tympanum of western portal. *Majestas Domini;* Virgin, St. John and seven Apostles; Angels; Visitatation; Scenes from Life of St. Loup, etc. L. W. P. phot.

1493. St.-Loup-de-Naud, (Seine-et-Marne). Western portal, northern jamb. Jeremiah, Queen of Sheba, St. Paul. L. W. P. phot.

1494. St.-Loup-de-Naud, (Seine-et-Marne). Western portal, trumeau. The Saint receives a precious Stone from Heaven; St. Loup. L. W. P. phot.

1495. St.-Loup-de-Naud, (Seine-et-Marne). Western portal, southern jamb. St. Peter, David, a Prophet. L. W. P. phot.

1496. Provins, (Seine-et-Marne), St.-Quiriace. Fragment of tympanum, now in west façade. *Majestas Domini.* L. W. P. phot.

1497. GASSICOURT, (Seine-et-Oise). Virgin (in wood). L. W. P. phot.

1498. VERMANTON, (Yonne). Western portal. Angels, Zodiac, Stoning of St. Stephen, two Prophets. L. W. P. phot.

1499. VERMANTON, (Yonne). Western portal. Angels, Zodiac, Elders, Simeon. L. W. P. phot.

1500. VERMANTON, (Yonne). Western portal, southern jamb. Simeon. L. W. P. phot.

1501. ANGERS, (Maine-et-Loire), Cathédrale. Tympanum of western portal. *Majestas Domini*. L. W. P. phot.

1502. ANGERS, (Maine-et-Loire), Cathédrale. Western portal, northern vous-. sures. Elders, Angels, St. Mark. L. W. P. phot.

1503. ANGERS, (Marne-et-Loire), Cathédrale. Western portal, northern jamb. Solomon; a Prophetess (?). L. W. P. phot.

1504. CHARTRES, (Eure-et-Loir), Musée Archéologique. Bust of Christ. A. K. P. phot.

1505. SENLIS, (Oise), Cathédrale. Western portal before restoration. From an engraving. L. W. P. phot.

1506. SENLIS, (Oise), Cathédrale. Western portal before restoration. From an engraving. L. W. P. phot.

1507. SENLIS, (Oise), Cathédrale. Western portal. Patriarchs, Kings of Judah, Prophets; Entombment, Resurrection and Coronation of the Virgin; St. John Baptist, Samuel, Moses, Abraham, Simeon, Jeremiah, Isaiah, David. L. W. P. phot.

1508. SENLIS, (Oise), Cathédrale. Jamb sculptures of western portal before restoration. St. John Baptist, Moses, Abraham, Simeon, David. F. M. S. phot. from cast.

1509. SENLIS, (Oise), Cathédrale. Head of one of the jamb sculptures, now in museum. A. K. P. phot.

1510. SENLIS, (Oise), Cathédrale. Western portal, north podium. February. L. W. P. phot.

1511. SENLIS, (Oise), Cathédrale. Western portal, detail of tympanum. Resurrection and Coronation of the Virgin. L. W. P. phot.

1512. SENLIS, (Oise), Cathédrale. Western portal, detail of voussures. Joshua, Deborah, Gideon, Jephthah, Samson, Eli; Solomon, Roboam, Abia, Josaphat, Joram, Ozias; Prophets. L. W. P. phot.

1513. SENLIS, (Oise), Cathédrale. Western portal, detail of voussures. Enoch, Noah, Abraham; Jesse, David, Saul; Isaiah, Prophets. L. W. P. phot.

1514. CORBIE, (Somme), Notre-Dame. Apostles; Coronation of the Virgin; the Virgin; St. John. L. W. P. phot.

1515. CORBIE, (Somme), Notre-Dame. Trumeau of western portal. The Virgin. L. W. P. phot.

1516. VENDÔME, (Loir-et-Cher), La Trinité. Statue at crossing. Gabriel of the Annunciation. L. W. P. phot.

1517.   VENDOME, (Loir-et-Cher), La Trinité. Statue at crossing. Virgin of the Annunciation. L. W. P. phot.

1518.   VENDÔME, (Loir-et-Cher), La Trinité. Statue at crossing. L. W. P. phot.

1519.   St.-BENOÎT-SUR-LOIRE, (Loiret). Northern portal, detail of tympanum. Christ, St. Matthew, St. Mark. L. W. P. phot.

1520.   St.-BENOÎT-SUR-LOIRE, (Loiret). Tympanum of northern portal, detail. Christ, St. John, St. Luke. L. W. P. phot.

1521.   St.-BENOÎT-SUR-LOIRE, (Loiret). Northern portal, detail of lintel. Translation of the relics of St. Benedict; Children resuscitated. L. W. P. phot.

1522.   St.-BENOÎT-SUR-LOIRE, (Loiret). Northern portal, detail of lintel. Child resuscitated; Translation of Relics of St. Benedict; an Angel. L. W. P. phot.

1523.   St.-BENOÎT-SUR-LOIRE, (Loiret). Northern portal, detail of voussures. St. John, St. Peter, Angels. L. W. P. phot.

1524.   St.-BENOÎT-SUR-LOIRE, (Loiret). Northern portal, western voussures. Apostles, Angels. L. W. P. phot.

1525.   St.-BENOÎT-SUR-LOIRE, (Loiret). Northern portal, detail of eastern jamb. L. W. P. phot.

1526.   St.-BENOÎT-SUR-LOIRE, (Loiret). Northern portal, detail of eastern jamb. L. W. P. phot.

1527.   St.-BENOÎT-SUR-LOIRE, (Loiret). Northern portal, detail of western jamb. L. W. P. phot.

1411. BEAUVAIS, (Oise), Basse-Oeuvre. Western portal, detail. Stoedtner phot.

1412. LE MANS, (Sarthe), La Couture. Relief in northern wall. Christ. A. K. P. phot.

1413. ETAMPES, (Seine-et-Oise), St.-Basile. Archivolts of western portal. The Last Judgment. L. W. P. phot.

1414. St.-Benoît-sur-Loire, (Loiret). Capital of narthex. Seven Martyrs. L. W. P. phot.

1415. St.-Beno t-sur-Loire, (Loiret). Capital of narthex. Apotheosis of St. Martin. L. W. P. phot.

1416. St.-Benoît-sur-Loire, (Loiret). Capital of narthex. Annunciation; Infant
Christ and St. Joseph; Visitation; Christ in Temple. L. W. P. phot.

1417. St.-Benoît-sur-Loire, (Loiret). Capital of narthex. Scenes from the Apocalypse. L. W. P. phot.

1418. St.-Benoît-sur-Loire, (Loiret). Capital of choir. A. K. P. phot.
1419. St.-Benoît-sur-Loire, (Loiret). Capital of narthex. The Horsemen of the
Apocalypse. L. W. P. phot.

1420. St.-Benoît-sur-Loire, (Loiret). Capital of triforium. St. Benedict, Hugh, the Virgin. Giraudon phot. from cast.

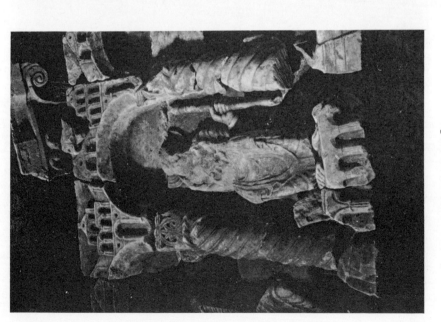

1421. St.-Benoît-sur-Loire, (Loiret). Fragments of altar-frontal. St. James.
       A. K. P. phot.
1422. St.-Benoît-sur-Loire, (Loiret). Fragments of altar-frontal St. James, an
       Apostle. A. K. P. phot.

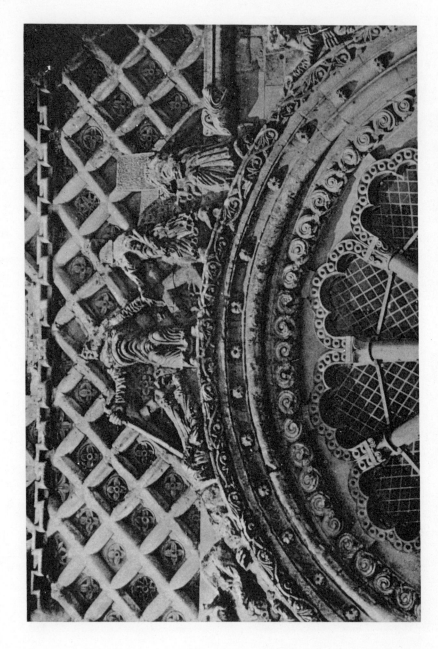

1423. Beauvais, (Oise), St.-Etienne. Northern transept, detail of rose. The Wheel of Fortune. F. M. S. phot.

1424. BEAUVAIS, (Oise), St.-Etienne. Northern transept, detail of rose. The Wheel of Fortune. F. M. S. phot.

1425. CHÂTEAUDUN, (Eure-et-Loir), La Madeleine. Northern façade, according to the drawing made for Montfaucon. B.-A. phot.

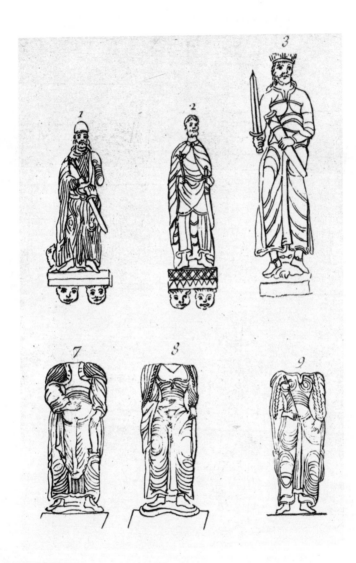

1426. CHÂTEAUDUN, (Eure-et-Loir), La Madeleine. Sculptures of northern façade, according to a drawing made for Montfaucon. B.-A. phot.

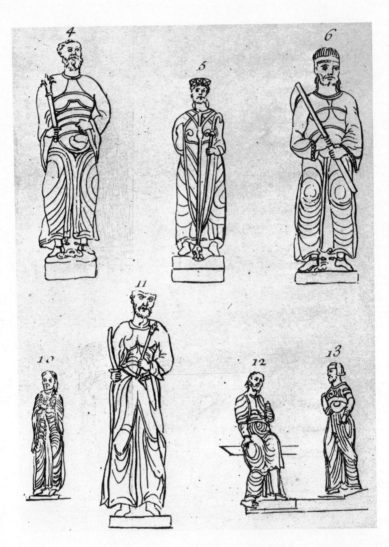

1427. Châteaudun, (Eure-et-Loir), La Madeleine. Sculptures of northern façade, according to a drawing made for Montfaucon. B.-A. phot.

1428. CHÂTEAUDUN, (Eure-et-Loir), La Madeleine. Southern portal, archivolt.
L. W. P. phot.

1429. Chȧteaudun, (Eure-et-Loir), La Madeleine. Southern portal, detail of voussures. L. W. P. phot.

1430. CHÂTEAUDUN, (Eure-et-Loir), La Madeleine. Southern portal, detail of voussures. L. W. P. phot.

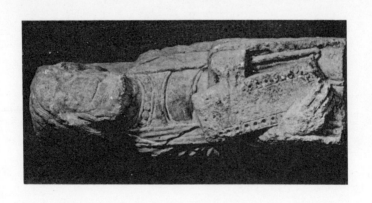

1431. ST.-QUENTIN-LÈS-BEAUVAIS, (Oise). Sculptured colonnette now in Beauvais
        museum. A. K. P. phot.

1432. ST.-QUENTIN-LÈS-BEAUVAIS, (Oise). Sculptured colonnette now in Beauvais
        museum. A. K. P. phot.

1433 ST.-QUENTIN-LÈS-BEAUVAIS, (Oise). Sculptured colonnette now in Beau-

1434. BRIARE, (Loiret). Fragment of altar-frontal now in Musée Historique,
Orléans. L. W. P. phot.

1437. St.-Denis, (Seine), Abbaye. Western façade, northern portal. Detail of voussures. Moses, David. L. W. P. phot.

1438. St.-Denis, (Seine), Abbaye. Western façade, northern portal, detail of socle. Aquarius. L. W. P. phot.

1439. St.-Denis, (Seine), Abbaye. Western façade, detail of central portal. The
Last Judgment. L. W. P. phot.

1440.   St.-Denis, (Seine), Abbaye. Western façade, central portal, northern voussures. The Elders, the Last Judgment. F. M. S. phot.

1441. ST.-DENIS, (Seine), Abbaye. Western façade, central portal, northern jamb. A foolish Virgin. F. M. S. phot.

1442. ST.-DENIS, (Seine), Abbaye. Western façade, central portal, southern jamb. A wise Virgin. L. W. P. phot.

1443. St.-Denis, (Seine), Abbaye. Western façade, southern portal, northern jamb. November and December. F. M. S. phot.

1444. St.-Denis, (Seine), Abbaye. Western façade, southern portal, southern jamb. February and January. F. M. S. phot.

1445. St.-Denis, (Seine), Abbaye. Destroyed sculptures of west façade, southern portal, from Montfaucon's drawings. Moses and a Prophet. B.-A. phot.

1446. ST.-DENIS, (Seine), Abbaye. Destroyed jamb sculpture of western façade,
        from Montfaucon's drawing. B.-A. phot.

1447. ST.-DENIS, (Seine), Abbaye. Destroyed jamb sculpture of western façade,
        from Montfaucon's drawing. B.-A. phot.

1448. St.-Denis, (Seine), Abbaye. Destroyed jamb sculpture of western façade, from Montfaucon's drawing. B.-A. phot.

1449. St.-Denis, (Seine), Abbaye. Destroyed jamb sculpture of western façade, from Montfaucon's drawing. B.-A. phot.

1450. ST.-DENIS, (Seine), Abbaye. Destroyed jamb sculpture of western façade,
       from Montfaucon's drawing. B.-A. phot.

1451. ST.-DENIS, (Seine), Abbaye. Destroyed jamb sculpture of western façade,
       from Montfaucon's drawing. B.-A. phot.

1452. St.-Denis, (Seine), Abbaye. Destroyed jamb sculpture of western façade, from Montfaucon's drawing. B.-A. phot.

1453. St.-Denis, (Seine), Abbaye. Destroyed jamb sculpture of western façade, from Montfaucon's drawing. B.-A. phot.

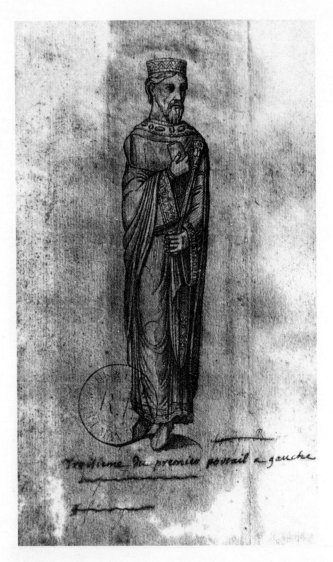

1454. ST.-DENIS, (Seine), Abbaye. Western façade, northern portal, destroyed jamb figure, from Montfaucon's drawing. B.-A. phot.

1455. St.-Denis, (Seine), Abbaye. Destroyed jamb sculpture of western façade, from Montfaucon's drawing. B.-A. phot.

1456. St.-Denis, (Seine), Abbaye. Destroyed jamb sculpture of western façade, from Montfaucon's drawing. B.-A. phot.

1457. St.-Denis, (Seine), Abbaye. Destroyed jamb sculptures of western façade, from Montfaucon's drawing. B.-A. phot.

1458.   PARIS, Musée du Louvre.   Heads.   Giraudon phot.

1459.   PARIS, Musée du Louvre.   Heads.   Giraudon phot.

1460. ETAMPES, (Seine-et-Oise), Notre-Dame. Southern portal. Angels, Prophets, Elders; Ascension; Birth of Christ; Precursors of Christ. L. W. P. phot.

1461. ETAMPES, (Seine-et-Oise), Notre-Dame. Southern portal, western spandrel. A Prophet an Angel. Prophets. Elders. L. W. P. phot.

1462. ETAMPES, (Seine-et-Oise), Notre-Dame. Tympanum of southern portal.
Prophets, Elders, Ascension. B.-A. phot.

1463. ETAMPES, (Seine-et-Oise), Notre-Dame. Southern portal, western jamb.
Esther, Moses, Melchisedek. B.-A. phot.

1464. ETAMPES, (Seine-et-Oise), Notre-Dame. Southern portal, eastern jamb.
David, Solomon, the Queen of Sheba. B.-A. phot.

1465. ETAMPES, (Seine-et-Oise), Notre-Dame. Statue now in chapel. St. Peter.
      B.-A. phot.
1466. ETAMPES, (Seine-et-Oise), Notre-Dame. Statue now in chapel. St. Paul.
      B.-A. phot.

1467. CORBEIL, (Seine-et-Oise), Notre-Dame. Jamb sculpture now in Louvre.
The Queen of Sheba. Restored. Stoedtner phot.

1468. CORBEIL, (Seine-et-Oise), Notre-Dame. Jamb sculpture, now in Louvre.
Solomon. Restored. Stoedtner phot.

1469. La Celle Bruère, (Cher). Relief of façade. L. W. P. phot.
1470. La Celle Bruère, (Cher). Relief of façade. L. W. P. phot.

1471. COULOMBS, (Eure-et-Loir). Sculptured column now in Louvre. The Sleep of the Magi. F. M. S. phot.

1472.   Coulombs, (Eure-et-Loir).   Sculptured column now in Louvre.   F. M. S.
     phot.

1473. COULOMBS, (Eure-et-Loir). Sculptured column now in Louvre. F. M. S. phot.

1474. IVRY-LA-BATAILLE, (Eure), Abbaye. Western portal. Patriarchs, Angels, Elders, Virtues. L. W. P. phot.

1475. Ivry-la-Bataille, (Eure), Abbaye. Western portal, detail of voussures. Angels. L. W. P. phot.

1476. Ivry-la-Bataile, (Eure), Abbaye. Western portal, detail of voussures. Elders, Angels. L. W. P. phot.

1477. Ivry-la-Bataille, (Eure), Abbaye. Western portal. Detail of voussures.
L. W. P. phot.

1478. Ivry-la-Bataille, (Eure), Abbaye. Western portal, southern jamb. The Queen of Sheba. L. W. P. phot.

1479. Véreaux, (Cher). Southern jamb of western portal. L. W. P. phot.
1480. Véreaux, (Cher). Northern jamb of western portal. L. W. P. phot.

1481. Véreaux, (Cher). Southern jamb of western portal, detail. L. W. P. phot.

1482. MERVILLIERS, (Eure-et-Loir). Tympanum of southern portal. A Knight doing Fealty to St. Poragie. L. W. P. phot.

1483. MERVILLIERS, (Eure-et-Loir). Tympanum of southern portal. A Knight doing Fealty to St. Poragie. L. W. P. phot.

1484. PARIS, Musée du Louvre. Virgin in wood. Giraudon phot.

1485. CARRIÈRE-ST.-DENIS, (Seine-et-Oise). Altar-frontal now in Louvre. Annunciation; Virgin; Baptism. Giraudon phot.

1486. CARRIÈRE-ST.-DENIS, (Seine-et-Oise). Altar-frontal, now in Louvre, detail.
The Virgin. Giraudon phot.

1487. CHÂLONS-SUR-MARNE, (Marne), Notre-Dame. Fragment of pier, now in
Louvre. Crusaders. B.-A. phot.

1488. PARIS, Ste. Geneviève. Capital now in Louvre. Daniel and the Lions.
F. M. S. phot.

1489. Issy, (Seine). Relief now in garden of priest's house. *Majestas Domini.*
L. W. P. phot.

1490. PROVINS, (Seine-et-Marne), St.-Ayoul. Western portal, tympanum and voussures. Angels, Elders, Seraphim, the Blessed, the Damned; *Majestas Domini*. L. W. P. phot.

1491. Provins, (Seine-et-Marne), St.-Ayoul. Western portal, southern jamb.
L. W. P. phot.

1492. St.-Loup-de-Naud, (Seine-et-Marne). Tympanum of western portal. *Majestas Domini*; Virgin, St. John and seven Apostles; Angels; Visitation; Scenes from Life of St. Loup, etc. L. W. P. phot.

1493. ST.-LOUP-DE-NAUD, (Seine-et-Marne). Western portal, northern jamb.
Jeremiah, Queen of Sheba, St. Paul. L. W. P. phot.

1494. ST.-LOUP-DE-NAUD, (Seine-et-Marne). Western portal, trumeau. The
Saint receives a precious Stone from Heaven; St. Loup. L. W. P.
phot.

1495. ST.-LOUP-DE-NAUD, (Seine-et-Marne). Western portal, southern jamb. St. Peter, David, a Prophet. L. W. P. phot.

1496.   PROVINS, (Seine-et-Marne), St.-Quiriace. Fragment of tympanum, now in
west façade. *Majestas Domini*. L. W. P. phot.

1497. GASSICOURT, (Seine-et-Oise). Virgin (in wood). L. W. P. phot.

1498. Vermanton, (Yonne). Western portal. Angels, Zodiac, Stoning of St. Stephen, two Prophets. L. W. P. phot.

1499. Vermanton, (Yonne). Western portal. Angels, Zodiac, Elders, Simeon. L. W. P. phot.

1500. Vermanton, (Yonne). Western portal, southern jamb. Simeon. L. W. P. phot.

1501. ANGERS, (Maine-et-Loire), Cathédrale. Tympanum of western portal. *Majestas Domini*. L. W. P. phot.

1502. ANGERS, (Maine-et-Loire), Cathédrale. Western portal, northern voussures. Elders, Angels, St. Mark. L. W. P. phot.

1503. Angers, (Marne-et-Loire), Cathédrale. Western portal, northern jamb.
Solomon; a Prophetess (?). L. W. P. phot.

1504. CHARTRES, (Eure-et-Loir), Musée Archéologique. Bust of Christ. A. K. P.
phot.

1505. SENLIS, (Oise), Cathédrale. Western portal before restoration. From an
engraving. L. W. P. phot.

1506. Senlis, (Oise), Cathédrale. Western portal before restoration. From an
engraving. L. W. P. phot.

1507. SENLIS, (Oise), Cathédrale. Western portal. Patriarchs, Kings of Judah, Prophets; Entombment, Resurrection and Coronation of the Virgin; St. John Baptist, Samuel, Moses, Abraham, Simeon, Jeremiah, Isaiah, David. L. W. P. phot.

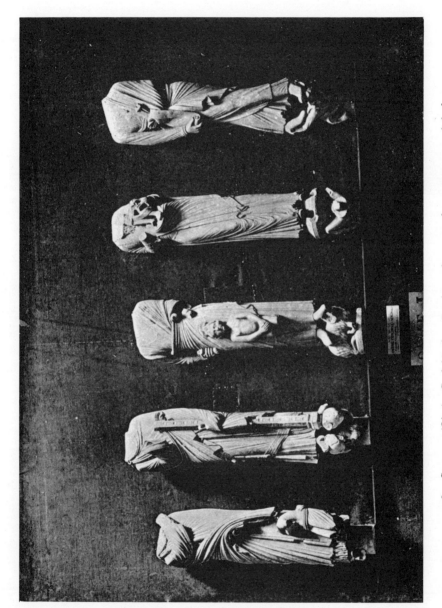

1508. SENLIS, (Oise), Cathédrale. Jamb sculptures of western portal before restoration. St. John Baptist, Moses, Abraham, Simeon, David. F. M. S. phot. from cast.

1509. SENLIS, (Oise), Cathédrale. Head of one of the jamb sculptures, now in museum. A. K. P. phot.

1510. SENLIS, (Oise), Cathédrale. Western portal, north podium. February.
L. W. P. phot.

1511. SENLIS, (Oise), Cathédrale. Western portal, detail of tympanum. Resurrection and Coronation of the Virgin. L. W. P. phot.

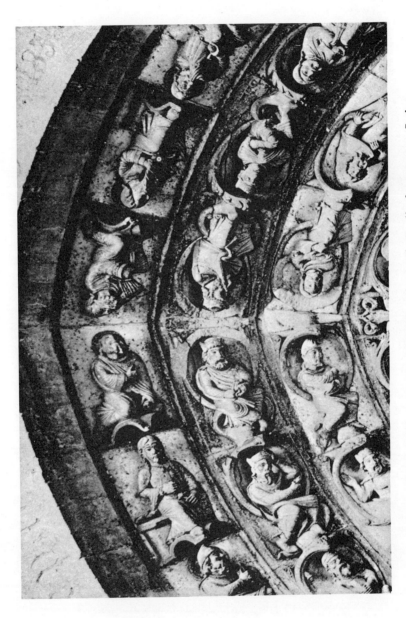

1512. SENLIS, (Oise), Cathédrale. Western portal, detail of voussures. Joshua, Deborah, Gideon, Jephthah, Samson, Eli; Solomon, Roboam, Abia, Josaphat, Joram, Ozias; Prophets. L. W. P. phot.

1513. SENLIS, (Oise), Cathédrale. Western portal, detail of voussures. Enoch,
Noah, Abraham; Jesse, David, Saul; Isaiah, Prophets. L. W. P. phot.

1514.   CORBIE, (Somme), Notre-Dame. Apostles; Coronation of the Virgin; the
Virgin; St. John. L. W. P. phot.

1515. CORBIE, (Somme), Notre-Dame. Trumeau of western portal. The Virgin.
L. W. P. phot.

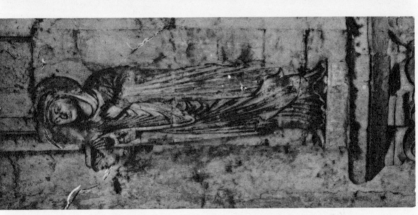

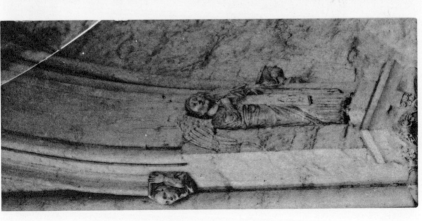

1516. VENDÔME, (Loir-et-Cher), La Trinité. Statue at crossing. Gabriel of the
Annunciation. L. W. P. phot.

1517. VENDOME, (Loir-et-Cher), La Trinité. Statue at crossing. Virgin of the
Annunciation. L. W. P. phot.

1518. VENDÔME, (Loir-et-Cher), La Trinité. Statue at crossing. L. W. P. phot.

1519. ST.-BENOÎT-SUR-LOIRE, (Loiret). Northern portal, detail of tympanum.
Christ, St. Matthew, St. Mark. L. W. P. phot.

1520. St.-Benoît-sur-Loire, (Loiret). Tympanum of northern portal, detail.
Christ, St. John, St. Luke. L. W. P. phot.

1521. ST.-BENOÎT-SUR-LOIRE, (Loiret). Northern portal, detail of lintel. Translation of the relics of St. Benedict; Children resuscitated. L. W. P. phot.

1522. St.-Benoît-sur-Loire, (Loiret). Northern portal, detail of lintel. Child resuscitated; Translation of Relics of St. Benedict; an Angel. L. W. P. phot.

1523. ST.-BENOÎT-SUR-LOIRE, (Loiret). Northern portal, detail of voussures. St.
John, St. Peter, Angels. L. W. P. phot.

1524. ST.-BENOÎT-SUR-LOIRE, (Loiret). Northern portal, western voussures. Apostles, Angels. L. W. P. phot.

1525. St.-Benoît-sur-Loire, (Loiret). Northern portal, detail of eastern jamb.
L. W. P. phot.

1526. St.-Benoît-sur-Loire, (Loiret). Northern portal, detail of eastern jamb.
L. W. P. phot.

1527. ST.-BENOÎT-SUR-LOIRE, (Loiret). Northern portal, detail of western jamb.
L. W. P. phot.